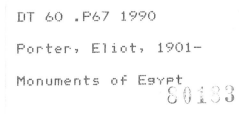

Monuments of Egypt

FRONTISPIECE: Isis (right) guiding Queen Nefertari, entrance room, Tomb of Nefertari (Tomb 66), Valley of the Queens, West Thebes.

Monuments of Egypt
Eliot Porter

Text by Wilma Stern

University of New Mexico Press, Albuquerque

LIBRARY OF CONGRESS CATALOGING-IN-PUBLICATION DATA

Porter, Eliot, 1901.
    Monuments of Egypt / Eliot Porter ; essay by Wilma Stern.—1st
ed.
     p.   cm.
    Includes bibliographical references (p.
    ISBN 0–8263–1232–2
    1. Egypt—Antiquities—Pictorial works.   2. Monuments—
Egypt—Pictorial works.   3. Egypt—Description and travel—1981
—Views. 4. Egypt—Antiquities.   5. Monuments—Egypt.
I. Stern, Wilma, 1940– . II. Title.
DT60.P67   1990
779'.9932—dc20   90–12871
                                      CIP

Monuments of Egypt was designed by Eleanor Caponigro.
The text was set by Michael and Winifred Bixler
in Monotype Joanna which was designed by Eric Gill.
Deborah Reade drew the map of Egypt.
The separations were made by Laser Images, Inc.
The book was printed by Land O'Sun
and bound by Roswell Bookbinding.
Grateful acknowledgment is made to the University of Chicago Press
for permission to quote from Herodotus, translated by David Grene.
Copyright © 1987 by the University of Chicago Press.

University of New Mexico Press
ISBN 0–8263–1232–2

Contents

Chronology

Selected List of Pharaohs

PREDYNASTIC
ca. 4800–3100 B.C.

EARLY DYNASTIC
Dynasties I–II
ca. 3100–2680 B.C.

OLD KINGDOM
Dynasty III
ca. 2680–2590 B.C.
Djoser
Dynasty IV
ca. 2590–2470 B.C.
Cheops (Khufu)
Chephren (Khafre)
Mycerinus (Menkaure)
Dynasty V
ca. 2470–2320 B.C.
Unas
Dynasty VI
ca. 2320–2160 B.C.

FIRST INTERMEDIATE PERIOD
Dynasties VII–X
ca. 2160–2040 B.C.

MIDDLE KINGDOM
Dynasty XI
ca. 2133–1991 B.C.
Dynasty XII
ca. 1991–1786 B.C.

SECOND INTERMEDIATE PERIOD
Dynasties XIII–XVII
ca. 1786–1580 B.C.

NEW KINGDOM
Dynasty XVIII
ca. 1580–1304 B.C.
Amenhotep I
Thutmose I
Thutmose II
Hatshepsut
Thutmose III
Amenhotep III
Amenhotep IV (Akhenaten)
Tutankhamen
Ay
Horemheb
Dynasty XIX
ca. 1304–1200 B.C.
Ramesses I
Sety I
Ramesses II
Merenptah
Sety II
Dynasty XX
ca. 1200–1085 B.C.
Ramesses III
Ramesses IV–XI

THIRD INTERMEDIATE PERIOD
Dynasties XXI–XXV
ca. 1085–664 B.C.

SAITE PERIOD
Dynasty XXVI
664–525 B.C.

THE LATE PERIOD
Persian domination
Dynasty XXVII
525–404 B.C.

Independence from foreign rule
Dynasties XXVIII–XXX
404–341 B.C.

Second Persian domination
Dynasty XXXI
341–332 B.C.

Ptolemaic Period
332–31 B.C.

Roman Rule
30 B.C.–A.D. 395

Coptic Period
Late Second Century A.D.–A.D. 641

Arab Conquest
A.D. 641

Preface

To any traveler in Egypt with an interest in classical antiquity, there is a heady excitement in following in the footsteps of the great ancient tourists, from Herodotus to Hadrian. There was, in my case, the additional attraction of viewing many sites through the perceptions of Eliot Porter. Hunting to discover the exact viewpoints he had selected more than fifteen years ago, indeed being able, in many cases, to determine not only where he stood but the time of day he had been at each place, lent great interest to a recent tour of the sites he had visited.

In the spring and again in the autumn of 1973, Eliot Porter traveled in Egypt at the invitation of Kenneth W. Kitchen, taking photographs to illustrate a book about the Pharaoh Ramesses II. These pictures constitute a chronologically and thematically broad view of ancient Egypt of significant artistic interest. They are used here as Dr. Porter intended, although not with the text originally planned.

I was privileged to meet Dr. Porter in Maine, in 1982, while visiting his son and daughter-in-law, the sculptor Stephen Porter and his wife, Marcie. It was Steve's suggestion that I talk to his father about preparing a text for his photographs of Egypt. In 1988, I visited Dr. Porter and his wife, Aline, at their home and studio near Santa Fe to select photographs for the present book. The initial choices were made in collaboration with Eleanor Caponigro, whose excellent taste and knowledge of Dr. Porter's work is thus responsible for more than the design of this publication. The text is intended as a brief framework that locates the photographs in a chronological, artistic, and cultural framework to make them intelligible to viewers interested in but not deeply familiar with ancient Egypt, much as a first-time tourist learns about Egypt.

I was able to follow Dr. Porter's path through Egypt in March 1989, through the assistance of the Department of Classics and the College of the Liberal Arts of the Pennsylvania State University, for which I am extremely grateful. This trip gained greatly from the companionship and knowledge of Joyce Haynes and the enthusiasm of fellow travelers Elinor and Bob McDade and Joyce Klepper. I am also grateful to Gerry Kadish of the State University of New York, Binghamton, for a day spent with him at the funerary temples of West Thebes and at the Valley of the Queens. I have been saved from many errors by Joyce Haynes and the helpful comments of two anonymous reviewers. Those that remain are my own. I also extend my thanks to the University of New Mexico Press, and especially their editor, Dana Asbury.

Wilma Stern
University Park, 1990

Introduction

ELIOT PORTER is widely recognized as a leader in color photography of the natural environment. He pioneered the use of dye-transfer printing as a serious artistic medium at a time when black and white was considered the appropriate artistic medium for photographers. His photographs of birds, the West and Southwest United States, Maine, the Appalachians, China, Greece, Antarctica, Africa, Iceland, and the Galapagos Islands have presented these subjects with a clarity and quiet authority that subtly hides the acute selectivity and compositional balance that are always present in his work.

In his photographs of Egypt, Dr. Porter was not entirely confined by the parameters of the initial project, and the range of subjects he chose is revealing of his photographic vision. In all his work, he seeks out the significance of the natural environment as he finds it, probing its essence and its message for our time. In Egypt, it is as if he found in the architectural and sculptural remains an expression of the nature of that country more compelling and more profound than the landscape environment. Cultivated Egypt, limited south of Cairo to a narrow band on either side of the Nile River, has been constantly subject to human manipulation since its permanent settlement seven millennia ago, thus effectively erasing most traces of untampered nature. The construction of the Aswan High Dam, which has absolutely transformed the geography and ecology of Egypt and of its estuarine fisheries in the Mediterranean, is but the most recent and most profound of continuous efforts to traduce geographical reality in the Nile valley. One can say that there is virtually no "natural" environment in much of Egypt. Porter's selective view of Egypt implies that it is the evidence of human shaping, now most expressively visible in the monuments of architecture and sculpture preserved from antiquity, that reveals the true "nature" of that country.

In the few photographs where the surrounding landscape is incorporated into the composition, in the case of Memphis, Giza, and Deir el-Bahari, special considerations apply. Porter's view of Memphis shows the site under water, the flooding a reminder of the annual inundation of Egypt until the Nile was fully dammed, and of the impossibility of fully controlling nature even with modern technology. The photographs of the Giza pyramids and the surrounding desert are from selected vantage points that capture an area of sand devoid of all other traces of human activity. Resolutely non-picturesque, Porter's image of these great monuments is of powerful masses hunkered into an implacable landscape of sand and rock. By including the great arena of cliffs at Deir el-Bahari, rising above the courts and colonnades of the Temple of Hatshepsut, he explains the penetration of the rock face by the inner chambers of the architectural complex. But in his photographs of Abu Simbel, where a similar relationship of structure to living rock existed in antiquity, Porter concentrates only on the details. The moving of these great monuments to artificial sites for preservation from flooding by Lake Nasser, formed by the dam at Aswan, makes their modern setting meaningless in the context of his aesthetics. In every case, his aim has been to express the reality of the monument, not its site's appearance at a specific point in time.

Every photographer is confronted in Egypt with the challenge of expressing the scale of the monuments. Some insert human figures, often in native dress, to add a touch of the exotic while pointing up the massive size of the architecture. However, the human presence implies a transience that contradicts the sense of the eternal aroused by these ancient structures, and the modern Egyptian cannot serve well to express the reality of antiquities from which he is chronologically remote and culturally displaced. With the unending reserves of patience and careful management that he applies to photographs of the elusive bird, Porter included a subsidiary figure in only one case, a view of the entrance to the funerary complex of Djoser at Saqqara. Here, the human figure serves the compositional function of continuing the diagonal line of shadow initiated at the upper left of the photograph to a firm base at the bottom of the wall. The triangle created is repeated again at the upper right, and sets up a pyramid-like counter to the strong verticals of the facade.

Eliot Porter is not uninterested in human subjects when they constitute the essential character of a place for him. His pictures of China, where one is always conscious of being among one-fourth of the world's total population, include many figures; and occasionally, in other work, when the person was integral to his experience of the place—the portrait of Earl Brown in *Summer Island*, for example—they occur quite naturally. Thus the dignified and grave picture of his Egyptian guide at Karnak appears separately in its own right, not as an appendage in an architectural setting.

The power of scale in architecture and sculpture is communicated subtly, by composition. Distant space, which tends to diminish the apprehension of mass, is almost everywhere reduced by the selection of close viewpoints. In many cases, architectural elements are shown overlapping and sculpture is shown within its architectural setting, rather than against the landscape. Porter also concentrates on the texture of masonry surfaces through the manipulation of focus and close viewing distance. These devices bring the viewer to a direct experience of monumental scale and of the three-dimensional solidity of sculptural and architectural form.

Composition and color unite in an armature of balance and amplitude that project a mood of calm introspection. Compositions arise from the subject and are never contrived, trite, or nervous. The calm of a scientist's vision reminds us of Porter's training in medicine and his early research career. The dye-transfer process used by Porter allows for adjustments to bring the color into harmony with his acute visual memory of each scene. On the one hand, we accept the color as being completely natural, and on the other, when the photographs are seen as a collection, we sense the control that brings them into a unified harmony of tone with variations on the predominant hues.

In Porter's photographs of Greece, by contrast, the world of nature seen close at hand is integrated with the architectural views. Tufts of grass or rows of flowers spring up between the treads and risers of steps, poplars shade an *agora*, fragments of sky and distant landscapes express the interpenetration of nature and art in Greek architecture. In planning concept and in the shaping of masses and space, Greek architecture is deeply organic. The swelling *entasis* of a Greek column and the elastic volutes of the Ionic capital express the muscular balance of weight and support in Greek architecture just as the flexing of a muscle expresses force in human anatomy. By emphasizing the interweaving of structure and nature in his photographs of Greece, Porter leads the viewer intuitively to sense this naturalism.

Egypt is a fertile country. In antiquity, as now, especially along the web of drainage and irrigation canals in the Delta north of Cairo, luxuriant vegetative growth is supported. Indeed, it was the fertility of the Nile valley that first caused a concentration of population along its banks. The Egyptian architectural vocabulary is taken from natural forms even more directly than the Greek. The reed-like convex fluting of columns and bud and flowering lotus and papyrus capitals were derived very closely from botanical forms. But Porter's view of Egypt suggests an inhospitable landscape and a truer image of the essential character of Egyptian architecture and sculpture. Abundant trees and plants appear only in the views of ancient Memphis. In a few other cases, a green landscape can be seen far off in the distance, a mirage that is tantalizingly unreachable. By minimizing the changing, growth-filled world of nature in his photographs of Egypt, Porter expresses its power and permanence as he experienced it, conveying his perception through purely photographic means.

It is Porter's great achievement as a photographer that he finds, in each environment he explores, a way to communicate the deeper reality of the place. Yet his method is so subtle that we simultaneously accept each picture as the simple capturing of surface appearance. It is the integration of that surface and the inner reality that he creates with such apparent ease. In the end, we truly know the essence of every place we visit through his art.

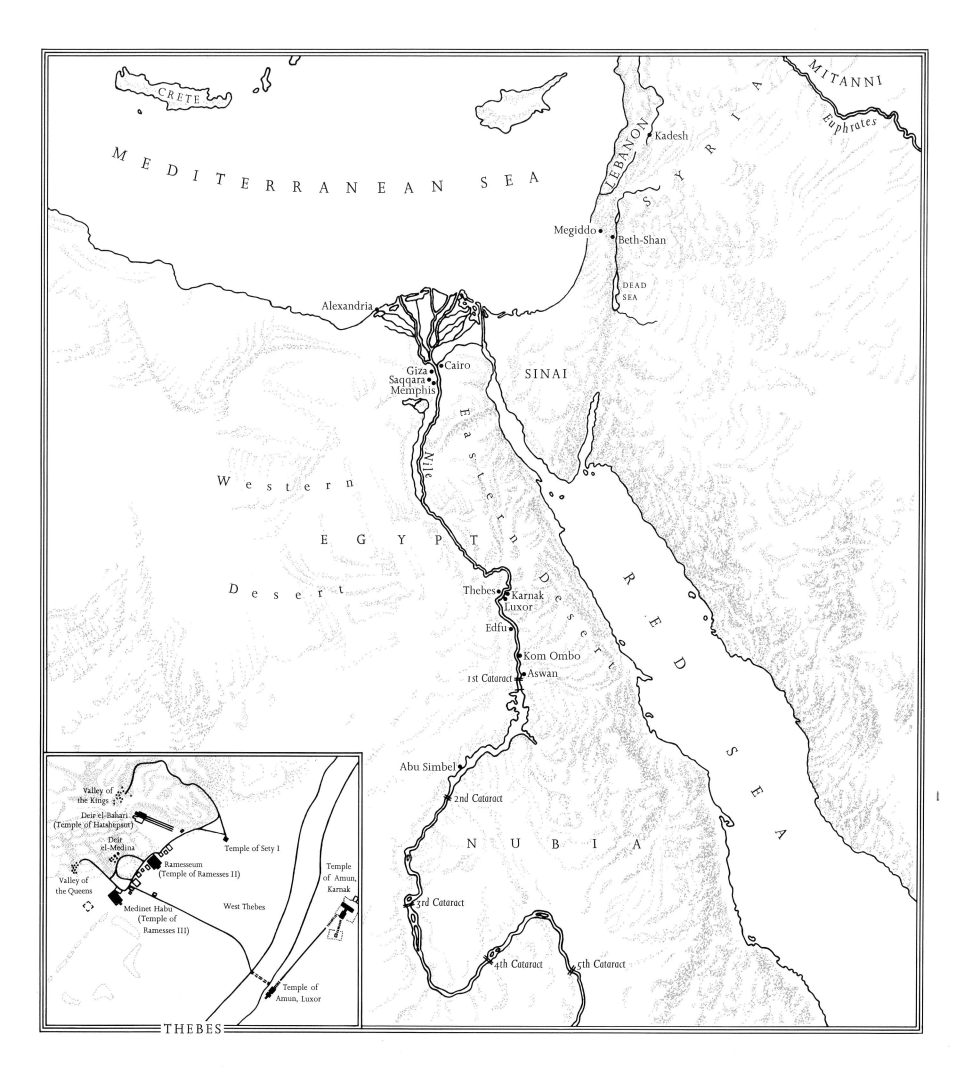

CRETE

MEDITERRANEAN SEA

LEBANON

SYRIA

MITANNI

Euphrates

Kadesh

Megiddo ● ● Beth-Shan

DEAD
SEA

Alexandria ●

SINAI

Giza ● ● Cairo
Saqqara ●
Memphis ●

W e s t e r n

E G Y P T

D e s e r t

Nile

E a s t e r n   D e s e r t

R E D   S E A

Thebes ● ● Karnak
Luxor
Edfu ●

Kom Ombo ●
1st Cataract ● Aswan

Abu Simbel ●

2nd Cataract

N U B I A

3rd Cataract

4th Cataract   5th Cataract

Valley of
the Kings
Deir el-Bahari
(Temple of Hatshepsut)
Deir
el-Medina
Temple of Sety I
Ramesseum
(Temple of Ramesses II)
Valley of
the Queens
Temple
of Amun,
Karnak
Medinet Habu
(Temple of
Ramesses III)
West Thebes
Temple of
Amun, Luxor

THEBES

Travels In Egypt

"Those obscure dynasties extended farther back than Rome, farther than Athens, back beyond the day when Achilles died before the walls of Troy. . . ."

Memoirs of Hadrian, MARGUERITE YOURCENAR

A TOUR OF Egypt tantalizes and provokes our drive to comprehend human history. Its monuments make a profound impression, yet they remain somewhat detached from the cord of human experience that ties us so much more closely to the ruins of Athens and ancient Italy. We respond warmly to the touching images of daily life in tomb paintings and figurines and are on familiar ground before Egyptian architectural forms and the idealized images of nature in its sculptures and reliefs. We are accustomed to them because the physical shape of our cultural roots at their earliest stage took form in Egypt. But a shadow slips before us as we confront the complex and profoundly alien nature of the religious beliefs that gave rise to these monuments. Egyptian beliefs, shifting and converging, animistic and abstract, visualized in animal or animalized human form, while progressively better understood by scholars, defy simple analysis. Descriptions of rituals and festivals inform us of external manifestations without bridging the gulf that separates us from the religion of the ancient Egyptians.

We approach Egypt today in much the same terms as ancient travelers did, asking similar questions and very often making the same observations as the Greek historians and geographers who traveled through Egypt over two thousand years ago. Since Roman times, we have erected obelisks, pyramids, and temples, appropriating the power of these forms while seeking to understand the beliefs that led to their creation. We seem to have penetrated Egyptian thought by building a transparent pyramid as a gateway to the heritage of artistic culture at the Louvre, but we remain uneasy before the serpents, vultures, and ibis-headed deities of the Egyptians preserved within. The concern with relating to the distant culture of Egypt persists because it was here that much of our intellectual and artistic life began to take form. We come the closest to the ancient Egyptians not before their monuments but in their private writings. The scraps preserved of their papyrus scrolls and jottings on flakes of stone and ceramic sherds preserve the experiences and emotions that we only sense in confronting the great religious and funerary monuments. These are the tenuous links that draw us so strongly to Egypt.

The sites of ancient Egypt most visited by tourists today are strung along the Nile from north to south in roughly the order in which they were built. The pyramids and tombs near Cairo in the funerary districts of Egypt's first capital at Memphis are the most visible remains of the earliest major phase of Egyptian history, the Old Kingdom. At Luxor, far upriver to the south, the magnificent structures of the New Kingdom were built in and near the ancient city of Thebes more than a thousand years later, when Egypt ruled an empire stretching from the Sudan to Syria. Even farther upstream, six hundred miles south of Memphis at Aswan, travel up the Nile was interrupted in antiquity at the border of Nubia by the granite boulders of the river's First Cataract, where today it is stopped by the high dam. North and south of Aswan are concentrated the later temples, including those of Kom Ombo and Edfu, built when Egypt was ruled by the Greek Ptolemies and then the Romans.

Egypt was most frequently ruled from Memphis, the administrative capital of the Old Kingdom, located about twenty miles southwest of Cairo. Its site falls near the transition between the Nile's triangular alluvial Delta in the north and the narrow valley of Middle and Upper Egypt to the south. This strategic location facilitated the unification of the country through military and political control of its

Fig. 1

Fig. 2

two, uneasily balanced regions. Even today, the contrast between Upper and Lower Egypt is marked, despite the changes in agricultural practices made possible by the high dam at Aswan. The fields of Lower Egypt stretch out across the Delta in the north. Roads linking town to town lace together Lower Egypt's new settlements set among the ancient network of cities and villages along the canals that distribute the Nile's water. In the south, where the roads and the narrow agricultural zone follow the single axis of the Nile, crops and trees are seen against a backdrop of dry and stony cliffs and desert. Here, the proximity of encroaching sand makes work and life more tenuous, and the watered fields along the river even more fruitful, sweet, and refreshing. The Greek geographer Strabo, who lived and studied in Egypt's Mediterranean port city, Alexandria, in the first century, described the shape of Egypt as an arm with outstretched hand, a narrow limb in the south with outspread fingers forming the streams the Nile followed across the Delta to the sea. With this hand, Egypt reached out to the eastern Mediterranean, establishing relationships with the cultural centers of the Near East, Asia Minor, and the Aegean.

The essential duality of the country was recognized throughout Egyptian history in the honorific titles and regalia of the king, who was simultaneously ruler of both lands. He is shown wearing a tapering white crown for Upper Egypt, a flat-topped red crown for Lower Egypt, or the double crown, a composite of the two. Through the dynastic period, the ruler's throne name was preceded with the *nesewt-bity* hieroglyphs, the sedge plant and the bee, signifying King of Upper and Lower Egypt. The same message was proclaimed by the vulture and cobra goddesses of Upper and Lower Egypt, which precede the third of the formal titles of the ruler. The theme was depicted in reliefs that show the Nile gods of Upper and Lower Egypt binding the sign "Unification" with papyrus, plant of the north and lotus, plant of the south. These fecund deities of mixed male and female traits convey the country's prosperity during the political unification of its two disparate regions. The insistent repetition of these formulae proclaims the critical importance of union. When centralized control failed, the country could more easily fall into disorder.

With the end of the prehistoric age at the turn from the fourth to the third millennium, around 3100 B.C., writing developed to meet the need for administrative record keeping that allowed appointed officials to measure, apportion, tax, and oversee the extended territory of Upper and Lower Egypt. Later, Egyptian geometry developed in the same way, as a result of the need to remeasure agricultural holdings after the annual inundation of the land. Literacy was limited to a small group of trained scribes, whose skills placed them high in the administrative bureaucracy that grew to govern the land and its people. The names of kings from this early stage onward were preserved in later lists. In the third century B.C., a scholarly priest, Manetho of Sebennytos, wrote an account in Greek of the history of the pharaohs that remains one of the sources for modern lists of the dynasties. Historians have organized the Third through the Twentieth dynasties into three major political stages, the Old Kingdom (ca. 2700–2200 B.C.), the Middle Kingdom (ca. 2050–1785 B.C.), and the New Kingdom (ca. 1580–1085 B.C.). These were separated by intermediate periods of political disruption.

The Old Kingdom, consisting of the Third through the Sixth dynasties, was a time of great creativity and innovation. During this period much that was essential to Egyptian religious belief, material culture, and political organization was brought into focus based on concepts that had their origins late in the preceding millennium. By about 3100 B.C., the earlier neolithic practices of burial in shallow, sandy graves and of house burial were replaced by tombs in designated cemeteries. The Egyptian belief in an afterlife involved an elaborate complex of burial practices. Ritualized preparation, mummification, wrapping, and entombment of the corpse ensured rebirth in the next world. Duplication of the dead through sculptured representation, and provision for an eternal afterlife by the interment of necessary objects or their representation in painted relief and offering scenes developed during the Old Kingdom to meet the requirements for this spiritual life of eternal bliss. It was believed that the spirit had three aspects, a transfigured spirit that dwelt in the heavens after death, a spirit (*ba*) that could fly back and forth from the dead body, and a vital force (*ka*) that could inhabit the tomb statue and take nourishment from offerings brought to the tomb by the funerary priest. Funerary rituals were critical to ensure the survival of these spirits that accompanied each person throughout his life. Only when the rituals were properly followed could

Fig. 67

the *ba*, which had the form of a bird or human-headed bird, fly back to the preserved body. Artistic representations of the dead and of offerings meant to augment the actual gifts brought to the tomb were essential to the continuity of the *ka*. The wonderful decorativeness and inventiveness of Egyptian art was, therefore, originally very secondary in importance to its role in providing for the afterlife.

The cemetery of Memphis at Saqqara was one of a series of burial zones in the desert on the west bank of the Nile, the direction of each day's setting sun. Pyramids and tombs, each complex visible from the next, rise from the top of an abrupt escarpment that hems in the fertile agricultural zone along the Nile. These areas are still much as the Greek geographer Strabo described about two thousand years ago, "a place so very sandy that dunes of sand are heaped up by the winds; and by these some of the sphinxes I saw were buried even to the head and others were only half visible; from which one might guess the danger if a sand-storm should fall upon a man traveling on foot . . ." (*Geography*, 17, 1, 32).

After a period of development during the first dynasties in which tombs grew in size, at the beginning of the Old Kingdom the creative and technical leap was taken to build these large structures of stone. The impermanent materials of mud brick for walls, reed bundles to support roofing beams, and thatch roofs were transformed into monumental scale and conception in the funerary complex of the Third Dynasty ruler, Djoser, at Saqqara. The inventive brilliance of his builder, Imhotep, was recognized by the Egyptians who later immortalized him as a deity, son of the creator god, Ptah.

Fig. 6

Imhotep designed the architectural forms still fundamental to Western building design—fluted column, capital, colonnade, and frieze—for the burial of Djoser. An encircling wall over a mile long and sixty-five feet high separates the sacred funerary complex from its surroundings. The wall's surface is articulated by a regular plan of alternating receding and projecting segments, each patterned with recessed panels, perhaps a reflection of the walls of the capital city, Memphis. Fourteen bastions are spaced along the wall, but only one has a true entrance to the funerary precinct. Its narrow doorway leads through a colonnade of convex fluted shafts, a stone version of supports formed from bundles of reeds. Overhead, rounded beams copy in stone the tightly packed logs that were used for roofing in

mud brick constructions. The colonnade opens out onto a brilliant expanse of ceremonial court. On its far side is a wall topped with a frieze of *uraei* or rearing cobra heads, the symbol of the power of the pharaoh and of the sun god, Re. The roll at the top of each recessed panel on the wall below this frieze derives from the shape of a mat door rolled up on a dowel. To the left of this wall is a shaft leading more than ninety feet deep to a tomb along the southern edge of the enclosure. Many theories have been proposed for the function of this tomb, among them that it served for the burial of the internal organs of the king that were removed during the mummification ritual. To the right of the entrance colonnade is a complex of false-fronted chapels dedicated to the district gods of Upper and Lower Egypt. Two structures beyond may refer to the ruler's palaces in the north and in the south, a reminder of his rule over a unified Egypt. Only the lower sections are preserved of their tall facades that were decorated with engaged columns, this time with concave flutes, the pattern the ancient Greeks would use two thousand years later. A frieze of tapered *kheker* (Egyptian for ornament) finials over the doorway of the House of the South translates into stone the shape of leafy reeds tied into clumps along the top of a palisade wall. The doorway is set off center. Perhaps builders had learned from trial and error that an additional support was needed at doorways in walls of less permanent materials, and conservatively carried over this practice when using a new material whose strength they had not yet learned to judge.

Fig. 8

The Step Pyramid of Djoser towers above the perimeter wall and dominates the north side of the open court. Its shape is an elaboration of the rectangular houselike structures with sloping walls that had been built over burials in the earlier dynasties. In these tombs, a narrow shaft led down to the underground burial chamber. This form of tomb, in modern times called a *mastaba* from the Arabic word for bench, was typical of burials in the north. In the south, piles of earth were erected over tombs, and it may have been from a synthesis of these two types of structure that the pyramid shape derived. In its early form, at Saqqara, the Step Pyramid of Djoser was first constructed as a mastaba with a square base. This original plan was then raised to a four-stepped pyramid of superimposed mastabas of diminishing size, and later given its final form, a rectangular plan with a higher six-step elevation. This imposing mass was

Fig. 10

built up of small blocks of limestone, a replacement for the mud bricks used for the mastaba tombs. At the base of its north side is an enclosed chamber, a *serdab*, that held a life-sized seated image of Djoser to provide a physical home for his *ka*, his spirit.

The stepped shape of this early pyramid gradually evolved to the true pyramid form found in the great triad of pyramids at Giza. The sheer size and power of these monuments is magnified by their placement near the front edge of the cliff that rises abruptly from the Nile plain. Their sobering impact also results from major improvements in the technology of their stone construction and design. The Pyramid of Cheops, the first and largest of the three, measures very near 756 feet along each side of its base. With its capstone and upper courses now missing, it is preserved to within about 31 feet of its original height of 481 feet. It is built of more than 2.3 million blocks that are much larger than those used in the Pyramid of Djoser. The largest weigh about fifteen tons. Its interior passageways and chambers are a marvel of structural ingenuity. The existing irregular surface of massive blocks was once cased with smooth-dressed white limestone. A portion of this facing remains at the cap of the second pyramid, the Tomb of Chephren, which was slightly smaller. The third pyramid, the Tomb of Mycerinus, smaller still, had a dark granite casing on its lower courses. These stones lie tumbled around its base. Next to it are the lesser pyramids of his queens.

Fig. 9

Each king's pyramid was but part of a large funerary complex that included a valley temple accessible to the Nile from a canal and a roofed causeway that led up the desert plateau to the mortuary temple adjacent to the pyramid. Deep within or under each pyramid lay the undecorated tomb chamber of the ruler, his remains originally enclosed in a monumental stone sarcophagus. The burial zone included mastaba tombs of members of the royal family and nobles and great funerary boats lying in pits. These ships of imported cedar, almost 150 feet long, may have been used for the funeral procession or were supplied for the dead ruler to accompany the sun god, Re, on his daily passage through the underworld, or both. The boat displayed on the south side of the Pyramid of Cheops was found with its coiled ropes and oars intact among the thousands of pieces.

Next to the valley temple before the Pyramid of Cheph-

ren, the Sphinx, about 238 feet long and 65 feet high, lies guarding the funerary precinct. It combines the body of a lion and head of the ruler, joining the fierce power of the animal to his divine authority. Most of the Sphinx was carved from a knoll left behind from quarrying. Other rock outcrops in the area have been wind eroded into similar recumbent shapes, suggesting that the design of the Sphinx may have been prompted by these naturally occurring forms. Over the millennia the rock has been amplified with masonry to maintain the paws and outer edges of its body.

Fig. 11

The Sphinx, like the other monuments of ancient Egypt, has suffered from erosion and surface deterioration caused by pollution and tourism. With the construction of the High Dam at Aswan, the Nile valley is no longer flooded each year, a process that previously carried fertilizing silt throughout the Nile valley and also flushed salts from the earth. The dam allows a controlled release of water throughout the year that has caused a significant rise in the water table in Lower Egypt. Capillary action pulls this moisture through the monuments, carrying the earth's natural salts to their surfaces, which crust and break off. Efforts to meet the modern threat to the survival of these monuments have their parallels in repairs made over two thousand years ago. The rounded top of a stone plaque is visible between the forepaws of the Sphinx. The inscription it carries commemorates a restoration during the New Kingdom by an Eighteenth Dynasty pharaoh, Thutmose IV, an ancient episode in the steady rebuilding work once again under way as portions of the stone break away.

Wind erosion, burial in shifting dunes of sand, neglect, and plunder had already brought these great monuments to a sorry state of disrepair by the New Kingdom. In the Nineteenth Dynasty, the zone of pyramids, funerary temples, chapels, and altars stretching from Giza in the north to beyond Saqqara in the south, fell under the supervision of Khaemwaset, the high priest of Memphis and fourth son of Pharaoh Ramesses II. He initiated restorations to the disintegrating monuments of Egypt's past heroic age and had inscriptions cut commemorating the work carried out under the authority of the pharaoh. An inscription of this type is cut into the vertical rock face along the north edge of the platform of the Pyramid of Chephren, recording restorations carried out by Maya, the pharaoh's chief builder.

Fig. 13

The overseer of works in the building named "Beneficent is Ramesses beloved of Amun in the great chapel of the nobleman," May, true of voice, son of the overseer of works Bak-en-Amun, true of voice, in Thebes (Signed:) the chief of sculptors, Pa-meniw, true of voice

The great size of the Fourth Dynasty pyramids was never again reached, but the goal of providing for the ruler's afterlife continued. In the Fifth Dynasty, a relief-decorated causeway was built from the valley temple to the mortuary temple at the base of the Pyramid of Unas at Saqqara. A granite gateway to the upper temple carries his names and titles inscribed by his successor, Teti. Mastaba tombs, which are present in the sacred precinct of each king's tomb, are lined up here next to the causeway. Like the mastabas at Giza, they contain false doors where the spirit of the dead can receive offerings and come into contact with the world of the living. A relief from the mastaba of Khenu, a later priest in the funerary complex of Unas, lays out its hieroglyphic message in a series of horizontal registers. The first row carries the distinctive cartouche of the King Unas. Below, in the second register, are the bee and the sedge, the cobra and the vulture, proclaiming Unas as the "King of Upper and Lower Egypt."

The Horus (name): "The one who causes the two lands to flourish."

The king of Upper and Lower Egypt, the one who causes the two ladies to flourish. The Horus of gold (name): "The one who causes flourishing."

For its eternity, the tenant of the Unas pyramid, the ka priest, the sole companion, the lector priest, the revered one before Unas, Khenu.

The lector priest, sole companion, revered one before his lord, Se-en-Unas, his son whom he loves.

Private mastaba tombs of the Fifth and Sixth dynasties provide for the afterlife of the dead through elaborate sculptured relief representations of the activities of daily life. Registers of low relief cover the walls of interior rooms cut out within the mass of the tomb. Scenes of hippopotamus hunting in the marshes of the delta show a richly inhabited world of bird, fish, and animal life, captured with intense observation of the natural environment. Scenes of sowing, harvesting, and the threshing of grain lay out the seasonal agricultural cycle that supports human life. The rich bounty of game and cattle are displayed for accounting before the deceased. He is presented the sustenance for the afterlife at an offering table richly piled up with bread and cakes.

The forms of nature are consistently transformed in Egyptian painting and sculpture. Repetitive elements that vary in nature are made uniform and reshaped into a geometric pattern. This stylization captures the stems of reeds in a marsh by a corduroy pattern of parallel vertical stripes, replicates the surface of water by repeated zigzags, and freezes the folds of cloth on a kilt into a row of concentric arcs. This convention enhances the clarity and decorativeness of the large wall surfaces of the tombs.

Human images in relief, painting, and sculpture in the round were designed on a grid. Craftsmen used a fixed system of proportion based on the subdivision of the cubit (20.6 inches). One cubit consisted of seven "palms," and each "palm" was subdivided into four "fingers." The size of each part was regulated by the "palm" module. For example, although the system varied at different periods, the length of the lower arm down to the tip of the thumb might be equal to six of these units, and the height from sole to hairline, eighteen units. The proportions of the smaller figures were also set by a grid, with its modular units smaller in proportion to the size of each individual figure. The size of figures may be determined not on the basis of their natural scale but in order to clarify the narrative or meaning of the scene. The pharaoh at war often towers over his own forces and those of the enemy. The owner of a tomb is commonly shown much larger than the other figures, or may be shown in radically different sizes in different scenes. Since size is used expressively, we often find that kings are disproportionately larger than subjects, masters larger than servants, and parents larger than children.

In Egyptian reliefs and paintings of the human figure, the parts of the body are shown from different viewpoints. The head is usually seen in profile, but the eye frontally. The shoulders and chest are viewed from the front, the stomach in three-quarter view, and the legs and feet in profile. This "aspective" technique presents each part of the body in its most distinctive or clearly defined shape in order to ensure its magical revivification in the next world. No attempt was made to define the transitions between these separate points of view. This approach, while arbitrary, leads to a constructed reality that provides great clarity.

Fig. 14

Fig. 12

Fig. 45

Egyptian images follow what Erik Iverson has called an "eternal reality" rather than the naturalism of the visual experience. Images communicate with intense clarity but not through consistent illusionism. On a practical level, Egyptian craftsmen trained in these methods produced work of high quality, and the systematization of procedure also made it possible for teams of craftsmen to produce very large-scale reliefs and paintings with stylistic uniformity.

Fig. 100

Two techniques of relief work predominated in Egypt. Low relief, the most common in the early periods, required the removal of the surface of the stone everywhere except the area within the outlines of the figures and the inscription. These protruding surfaces were then worked to create the interior planes and decorative elements of the figures. Sunk relief reverses the process. The flat surface of the stone is left intact, and only the area inside the contour of the figures is removed. Inner details are worked in relief within the depth defined by the contours, with shallow incision used for much of the decorative patterns. The outer contour of the figure must be cut deeply enough to create the depth needed for the interior modeling, and it picks up a line of shadow when lit by the sun at an oblique angle. The resulting strong linear contour is powerfully expressive and visually clear. As much less stone is removed, this technique is more economical than low relief and can be produced more quickly. There was no objection to the juxtaposition of low relief and sunk relief, and in some cases single rooms combined both methods. Sunk relief was typically used on the exteriors of buildings where the wall surfaces would be more subject to damage. Both techniques were used through all Egyptian periods, but sunk relief became particularly common in the New Kingdom and later, when enormous wall surfaces were covered with relief decoration.

Although its exterior is now a mound of rubble, the interior of the Pyramid of Unas is well preserved. A low, narrow shaft slopes down from the north side to a horizontal corridor that leads to an antechamber. A doorway in its west side opens into the burial chamber, which is lined with walls of limestone and alabaster. Its gabled roof is covered with stars cut into the surface and filled in with blue pigment. Except for the west end, the walls are completely covered from top to bottom with hieroglyphic inscriptions. These writings,

Fig. 15

the Pyramid Texts, are the earliest royal funerary texts that have survived. The inscriptions were originally filled in with blue pigment that is still preserved here and there. Of the 714 spells known from all the pyramids, 228 are found here. The texts are intended to elevate the king to the level of a major deity, may repeat the daily rites performed by the funerary priests of the ruler, and were intended to ensure his safe journey from this world to the next. The Pyramid Texts reflect on the netherworld, where it was believed the dead dwell among the gods, travels across the heavens, receives food offerings, or enjoys the pleasures of the afterworld. Later, some of these spells, edited and augmented, were written inside the sarcophagus of nonroyal personages as well. In the New Kingdom they developed into the Book of the Dead, which was often written on tombs, statues, coffins, and papyrus scrolls that were buried with the deceased.

The written Egyptian language, which survived for over 4,000 years after its beginnings in the fourth millennium B.C., is preserved in enormous quantities in stone inscriptions and writings on papyrus, pottery, linen, leather, and wood. Writing was central to the administrative organization of Egypt, and the high status of scribes is reflected in their frequent representation in reliefs and sculpture in the round. Stone inscriptions are devoted to dedications, cult hymns, and historical narratives, but Egyptian literature, preserved mainly on papyrus, is rich in variety and includes narratives, meditations, secular and religious poetry, love songs, and teaching materials such as sample letters and instructions for schoolboys. Much of what is preserved is thanks to the endless copying by students through which they learned to master the complexities of written Egyptian.

The earliest texts are written in a pictorial form, or hieroglyphic writing, whose outlines were organized into compositions of great beauty. Hieroglyphs, a Greek word meaning sacred sculptured (letters), are pictures of objects. The signs also represented the consonantal sounds of Egyptian speech. The absence of vowels in the writing system meant that many words were spelled the same way. Meanings were clarified by the use of nonphonetic determinative signs placed at the end of a word. Hieroglyphic inscriptions are written either vertically or horizontally. The individual signs face either right or left, and signs are occasionally moved out of sequence to form a more harmonious visual pattern. They are usually read against the direction they face. If, for example, the hieroglyphs face right, one reads toward the left. Hieroglyphs can be carved in low relief, incised,

Fig. 101

modeled in plaster, or painted on a flat surface in outline or silhouette. Within the expanse of inscriptions, some formulae and combinations of signs appear frequently and quickly become recognizable, among them the sedge and bee and the cobra and vulture. The bee, loaf, and two slanting parallel lines with the seated king wearing the red crown and holding flail and crook form the word *bity*, meaning King of Lower Egypt. The snake (*dj*) and loaf (t) together form the word *djet*, meaning forever or eternity. The hieroglyphic signs for the throne name and for the birth name of the pharaoh are surrounded with an oval formed by a rope coiled at the bottom. The rope never ends nor does the rule of the pharaoh. These ovals are called cartouches, from the French word meaning an ornate frame.

Fig. 61

A cursive form of writing, hieratic, developed from and in parallel with hieroglyphic. Hieratic, almost always written from right to left, was primarily used for literary works, administrative and legal affairs, and business records. A reed brush and ink were used to write on scrolls of paper made from strips of the stalk of the papyrus plant, on wooden boards which could be covered with stucco, on flakes of stone, or on pieces of broken pottery, called ostraca. Hieratic, "sacred writing," was so named by the Greeks because by the Late Period it was confined to religious use, having been supplanted for other purposes by demotic, a cursive form written with a reed pen that was used for literary, business, and everyday private affairs. Scribes are frequently pictured with their equipment, a long palette with holes for black and for red ink, a brush holder, and a water pot.

The sound of spoken ancient Egyptian is not certain. Some clues can be drawn from other ancient languages in which vowels are represented, such as Greek and Babylonian, and from Coptic, a form of Egyptian used from the Roman period on. The Coptic alphabet, which developed along with the spread of Christianity in Egypt, uses Greek letters plus seven characters derived from native Egyptian writing that represents Egyptian sounds for which Greek lacked a letter. Because written Coptic includes vowels, it provides some information, but its usefulness for the sound of earlier stages of Egyptian is limited by the very long history of the language during which changes certainly occurred.

The ability to read ancient Egyptian began to be recovered only in the early nineteenth century. One of the clues in deciphering Egyptian was the identification of cartouches in inscriptions. The Rosetta stone, which preserves one text written in three forms, hieroglyphic, demotic, and Greek, records the honors bestowed in 196 B.C. by the priesthood on King Ptolemy V Epiphanes, the only name that appears in the hieroglyphic section. A British linguist, Thomas Young, realized that the hieroglyphic text was not totally symbolic, but that it also represented sounds and was structurally related to the successor of hieratic, demotic, the form of one of the three versions of the inscription. Young was able correctly to derive several consonant sounds from the six cartouches naming Ptolemy in the hieroglyphic section of the Rosetta stone by comparison with the demotic inscription but was unable to make further progress.

The major breakthrough in the decipherment of hieroglyphic Egyptian writing was accomplished by a brilliant French scholar, Jean-François Champollion, who may have been aware of Young's publication of his preliminary work. Champollion used a pair of Greek and hieroglyphic inscriptions, found in 1819 near Aswan, that bear the cartouches of Ptolemy and Cleopatra. By matching the signs within the cartouches with their counterparts in the Greek inscription, he was able to determine the sound equivalent of several hieroglyphs and their demotic equivalents, assisted by the overlap of five sounds in the two names, *p, t, l, e,* and *o*. By determining the sound of the remaining signs in both names, and applying the results to cartouches of other kings and Roman emperors, Champollion was able to expand the list of known sounds and to determine many features of the Egyptian language. The results, published in 1824, laid the foundation for the modern study of ancient Egypt.

The analysis of language and study of the numerous documents that have survived, in the century and a half since this discovery, have provided significant insights into the complex world of Egyptian religious belief. Temple walls carry inscriptions listing the feasts and offerings of the ritual in an annual calendar. Details of the work force and endowments committed to some temples are also preserved in papyrus records. The rituals were dedicated to a diverse system of deities that gave concrete form to the cosmic forces that were perceived in the natural environment but whose energies could neither be controlled nor understood. In one of their myths of creation, the Egyptians thought of the earth as a mound that emerged from formless, watery chaos, through the primeval god of creation, Atum. Atum was visualized as a human, but also as a scarab bettle or as a serpent. Other deities were variously represented as humans, often with animal heads, or as animals.

Fig. 17

Each district throughout the country had a local deity, usually worshipped as a triad of god, consort, and offspring. Religious imagery is complicated by the practice of merging these local deities with the major gods and goddesses. Worship of the god Ptah developed very early at Memphis. Ptah, who was represented as a mummified man, was also a creator god and thus a god of those who create such as artists and craftsmen. He is elsewhere associated with the primeval mound and called *Ta-tenen*, the rising land. Sekhmet, the lion-headed daughter of Re, was the consort of Ptah, and also became a fierce goddess. Their son, Nefertum, has a human form with the head surmounted by a lotus flower.

Fig. 19

Fig. 25

Fig. 18

Fig. 62

Amun, the local god of Thebes, was represented as a human with a tall headdress of two falcon plumes. Assimilated with the sun god as Amun-Re, he became a supreme deity in the New Kingdom. The triad of Amun, his consort Mut, and their son, the moon god, Khons, was worshipped at temples in a huge complex at Karnak in Thebes, the religious center of Upper Egypt.

One of the foremost religious centers of Egypt was Heliopolis, a sun worship site located northeast of Cairo. Its sun god, Re, was represented as a falcon-headed man crowned by a sun disk sometimes encircled by a cobra. Horus, the son of Re, was represented as a falcon or as a human with the head of a falcon. Pharaoh, the incarnation of Horus, had divine power to protect the prosperity of the land. It was thought that at death the pharaoh becomes the god of the underworld, Osiris; his son, Horus, ascends the throne as the new ruler.

Fig. 16

Fig. 24

Some local gods and goddesses came to be widely revered when their town or district became elevated politically. The worship of Hathor, a goddess of love, joy, and fertility, was originally associated with the town of Dendera, north of Luxor in Upper Egypt. Temples and shrines were dedicated to Hathor throughout the land. She was represented as a human, a cow, or a cow-headed human. Her attributes include the *menat* necklace and the *sistrum*, a ritual curved rattle.

Fig. 21

Other amulets and emblems are widely represented in

Egyptian art. The most common of these is the *ankh*, which may originally have represented a sandal strap, the word for which contained the letters *a*, *n*, and *kh*. The sign was adapted to stand for a number of unrelated words that consisted of the same three consonants but different vowels. Among these is the word *ankh*, meaning life. A related symbol, the *tyet*, is the shape of an *ankh* with its cross arms extended and hanging down. This sign, the girdle tie of Isis, signified protection and well-being. The *djed* column, which takes its form from a lashed bundle of papyrus stalks, was originally thought of as the column that held up the sky. It later was associated with backbone or Osiris and signified endurance and stability. The *wedjat* is the whole or sound eye of Horus that warded off evil and illness. The scarab, *khepri*, a dung beetle, was a symbol of the rebirth and regeneration often associated with the rising sun. It was also the principal name of the youthful aspect of Re or Atum. The dung beetle lays its eggs in a ball of dung and sand. The breaking forth of the young was considered a parallel to the rebirth of a new day from the corruption and death of the night.

Fig. 28

Myths and legends helped individuals gain a sense of coherence and control over the world of chance and chaos. Some stories were enacted as religious observances, among them many legends about the murder and revival of Osiris. Osiris, god of the underworld, was also a god of vegetation. Although usually shown with natural skin, he was sometimes represented as black or green. Osiris was murdered and dismembered by his brother, Seth, who envied his power. Isis, the wife/sister of Osiris, searched for him, at length rescued him, and restored him with the power of the secret name of Re. Horus, their son, was selected by the gods to inherit the kingship. Seth sought revenge for being frustrated in his attempted murder of Osiris, and engaged in great battles with Horus. The mythical resurrection of Osiris reflected the annual rebirth of plants after the withering drought and heat of the dry season, but also gave voice to the hope of rebirth in an afterlife for humans facing the unknown beyond the grave. The battles between Horus and Seth related to the establishment of the legitimacy of the ruler and carried overtones of the conflict between cosmic order (the Egyptian *ma'at*) and chaos. Osiris, the god of the underworld, and Anubis, the jackal who guards the entry to the underworld, were frequently depicted in tombs. Osiris is represented cloaked in a shroud with crossed arms hold-

Fig. 26

Fig. 23

Fig. 22

ing a crook and flail. The pharaoh was also at times represented in the guise of Osiris.

Temples were built as an earthly house for the god, who resided in its inner sanctuary to which only the priesthood penetrated. Proper performance of ritual was ensured by records kept of the correct procedures in the temple library. Major features of the ritual were also inscribed on the walls of the temples. The gods were conceived as physical presences whose requirements were tangibly fulfilled in elaborate rituals by the priests. Their daily enactment focused on providing food and anointing and garbing the statue of the god.

In the New Kingdom and later, temple plans consisted of a similar repertoire of building elements placed along a central axis. Long avenues flanked by rows of sphinxes led to the entrance of many temples, occasionally connecting one temple precinct to another. At Karnak, these sphinxes were in the form of the ram of Amun protecting an image of Fig. 31 the Pharaoh Ramesses, under whom they were set up. The main entrance to the temple precinct was a towering entrance gate called a pylon. Their walls were usually covered with large relief decorations and inscriptions. Paintings and reliefs illustrate the huge staffs for banners that were set into their walls. In a painting from his tomb, Panehesi, a temple functionary in the time of Ramesses Fig. 37 II, makes an offering before the pylon of the temple of Amun-Re, which shows these flagstaffs projecting high above the gateway. The construction of major temples over many reigns could lead to a sequence of several pylons Fig. 54 spaced out along the temple plan. Colossal sculptures in the round and obelisks covered with dedication inscriptions Fig. 53 were often set before these pylons. The slender, tapering obelisks originated in a squat form in sun sanctuaries of the Fifth Dynasty. The small pyramid at their apex, the first point to be touched by the rising sun's light at dawn, was Fig. 50 thought to be a resting place for the sun god.

Behind the pylon was an open courtyard surrounded by a single or double row of columns that provided an open Fig. 57 gathering space before the series of halls that led to the inner sanctuary. The far colonnade of the courtyard served as a portico for the hypostyle hall, a large room filled with rows Fig. 30 of columns. The center rows of columns in the hypostyle hall were sometimes higher than the side rows, and the vertical walls between the two levels were filled with grat-

ings to let subdued light filter down into the forest of columns. Additional pylons and halls could follow along the same axis, or the columned hall could lead more directly to the inner sanctuaries and shrines of the temple.

Rooms for the preparation and storage of offerings surrounded the sanctuary, sometimes off a corridor that led around the outside of the shrine in a separate passageway. At the great temple of Amun at Karnak, additional temple complexes were built at right angles to the main plan, and these were extended through numerous pylons, courts, and halls of their own. Especially in the later periods, some temples were totally surrounded by an enclosure wall, both for protection and to demarcate their ritually purified area from the profane surrounding space. An additional shrine, the Birth House or *mammisi*, was built before the entrance pylon of the later temples. This shrine was dedicated to the birth and nurturing of the offspring of the deity and the consort to whom the sanctuary was dedicated.

During some festival celebrations, the statue of the deity was brought out for transport to neighboring shrines, but Fig. 52 otherwise it was not visible to the public. These images were carried on sacred boats that were kept in a bark shrine in the temple. One of the most important of these celebrations, the Festival of Opet, was held at Thebes each year during the second month of the Season of Inundation. The image of Amun was transported from his temple at Karnak to the shrine of his consort, Mut, at the Luxor Temple. Scenes from this procession are depicted in reliefs on the interior walls of the colonnade at Luxor. These festive parades of horses and of garlanded boats drew large crowds of onlookers.

The Greek historian Herodotus recounted his observation of a much later festival of the goddess of love, Bastet, who was given the form of a cat, that he came upon in Lower Egypt while touring the country in the mid-fifth century B.C.

When they travel to Bubastis, this is what they do: They sail thither, men and women together, and a great number of each in each boat. Some of the women have rattles and rattle them, others play the flute through the entire trip, and the remainder of the women and men sing and clap their hands. As they travel on toward Bubastis and come near some other city, they edge the boat near the bank, and some of the women do as I have described. But others of them scream obscenities in derision of the women who still live in that city, and others of them set to dancing, and others still, standing up, throw their clothes open to show their nakedness. This they do at every city along the riverbank. When they come to Bubastis, they celebrate the festival with great sacrifices, and more wine is drunk at that single festival than in all the rest of the year besides. There they throng together, man and woman (but no children), up to the number of seven hundred thousand, as the natives say. (II, 60; tr. David Grene, University of Chicago Press, 1987).

People celebrated even more solemn feasts, such as the annual Festival of the Valley at Thebes, with a procession across the Nile of the bark of Amun from Karnak to the temples of the west bank with feasting, music, and dance at the tombs of the deceased.

The five hundred years of the Old Kingdom ended with the close of the Sixth Dynasty. By then, Egypt's local nobles had grown in power at the expense of centralized authority. In this First Intermediate Period, from the Seventh through the Tenth dynasties, the country was not unified by a single ruler. There were periods of cultural and economic disruption at the outset and the end of this two-hundred-year span. About 2050 B.C., the rulers of Thebes, the capital of Upper Egypt, had consolidated their power and under its prince, Mentuhotep II, overcame Lower Egyptian rivals and took control, once more, of a unified land.

The two subsequent dynasties, the Eleventh and Twelfth, which constitute the Middle Kingdom, saw the extension of Egyptian interests farther south and into areas beyond the boundaries of the Nile valley. Nubia, up to the second of the six cataracts that interrupt the Nile between Aswan and Khartoum, was brought under control, and an expedition was mounted to the land of Punt, probably East Africa, one of the sources of incense. Relatively little of the major architectural undertakings of the Middle Kingdom are preserved. In the subsequent Second Intermediate Period, when much of Egypt was ruled by foreign invaders, these monuments served as a source of building materials or later fell into disuse and decay. The most extensive complex that is partially preserved is the funerary temple and tomb of Mentuhotep II at Deir el-Bahari, a series of colonnaded terraces approached by ramps surmounted by a relatively small pyramid.

There were significant cultural advances and developments in religious beliefs during the Middle Kingdom. Much of the sculpture of this period is of a high level of craftsmanship and displays an impressive individuality and sensitivity. New sculpture types were invented such as the "block-statue," a compact image that shows the head rising from a squatting, draped figure. Tomb paintings of the Middle Kingdom, of great interest but mostly poorly preserved, show evidence of contacts with the great Bronze Age civilizations of the Aegean. Egyptian literature is considered to have reached its highest level during the years of the Middle Kingdom. A belief that all Egyptians could enjoy an eternal afterlife through their own merits brought about an expansion in the production of funerary arts and supported a strengthened concept of morality.

This second period of stability lasted almost three hundred years, after which Egypt was affected by a migration that brought tribes down into the Middle East, displacing some of its population southward into Egypt. Manetho provided our name for these Semitic invaders, the Hyksos. They gradually infiltrated down into the Delta, and by about 1675 B.C. they controlled Memphis. The first Hyksos dynasties ruled simultaneously with gradually weakening southern rulers, some of whom ruled over several nomes and others over just a single town, and then they consolidated power as the Fifteenth and Sixteenth dynasties. The Hyksos left no monumental architecture that remains standing, but archaeologists are revealing their settlements. They were particularly active in the copying of literary and technical works that have survived. The Hyksos traded widely in the Near East and possibly conducted an embassy to the Bronze Age civilization of Crete, judging from the cartouche of the Hyksos King Khyan found on a jar lid at the main Minoan center at Knossos. The increased foreign contacts of the Hyksos period were a significant forerunner of the military expansionism of the subsequent New Kingdom, which began after the rulers of Thebes once more led a movement to unify the country.

The New Kingdom, initiated with the Eighteenth Dynasty about 1580 B.C., lasted just under five hundred years, as long as the Old Kingdom. During its three dynasties, Egypt reached its greatest international power and a peak of artistic and cultural creativity. With the energetic militarism that expelled the Hyksos rulers, Egypt's power reached to the Euphrates River for the first time. Expansion to the south extended Egyptian control to the region of the Third Cataract under Thutmose I and to the Fourth, on a permanent basis, by the reign of Thutmose III.

The personalities of the Eighteenth Dynasty and their monuments leave an indelible impression on the modern consciousness. Among them is Hatshepsut, the wife of Pharaoh Thutmose II. After the death of her husband during the minority of his son by a lesser wife, Hatshepsut acted as regent. She then usurped power and ruled as pharaoh, having herself represented in male garb. Hatshepsut constructed a great funerary temple adjacent to the Middle Kingdom temple of Mentuhotep II at Deir el-Bahari that follows the conception of its forerunner to the south. It consists of a series of colonnaded terraces reached by great ramps. The inner walls of the colonnades were decorated with colored reliefs depicting religious themes and the accomplishments of her reign, including a famous expedition she sponsored to the land of Punt. The structure enjoys one of the most dramatic sites in all Egypt, backed against a cove of steep cliffs.

Unlike its adjacent predecessor, the temple of Hatshepsut was not a tomb. Earlier in the Eighteenth Dynasty, the change had already been made in royal funerary practice to separate the tomb from the mortuary temple. Tombs were hidden away in deep valleys in the western desert across the river from Thebes. Narrow passageways and stairs led to chambers cut out of the rock, often with pillars left in place. After the burial, the entranceways were sealed and recovered, hiding the wealth of furnishings and offerings buried within. The royal funerary areas, the Valleys of the Queens and of the Kings, were protected by guards. The craftsmen who excavated and decorated these tombs were segregated in an isolated village in a vain attempt to prevent the plunder of their extraordinary wealth. The remains of the workers' town, Deir el-Medina, lie hidden away in the Theban hills. They survived under windblown sand because they had few valuables to be plundered and were safe from erosion beyond the flood plain of the Nile. About three hundred residents occupied the seventy homes lined up along the main street that doglegs through the town. The houses were long and narrow, with the vestibule set below the level of the street. The main room beyond had a higher roof supported by columns. Cellars were sometimes dug under this larger room, and the family's most valuable possessions could be stored safely in these spaces. The name of the owner was painted on the door post of the entrance. In a few cases, the occupant of a house can be matched with names in the extensive written records from the village that are preserved in papyrus and on pieces of limestone and ceramic. Accounts of the delivery of rations, of work accomplished, and of notes and messages reveal the organization of the work force and daily life of this isolated town. The craftsmen were separated into two teams, each under the administration of a foreman. During their work "weeks," the tomb diggers, sculptors, and painters lived in crude huts built above the area where the royal tombs were cut out of the rock.

A glimpse of the workshop of these funerary craftsmen is preserved in the tomb of the sculptor Ipuy. The making of wooden tomb furnishings is shown from the felling of a tree to the display of the finished equipment. At the bottom, workmen clamber over the elaborate catafalque and shrine they are preparing for the burial. A bedstead with curved headrest is tucked beneath the bier. In the register above, finishing touches are applied to a funerary mask and mummy cases, while at top a lively forester cuts down a tree for lumber. Arrayed along the registers are the elaborate chairs, folding stools, tables, and offerings being prepared for a great burial. At Deir el-Medina, excavations have recovered traces of painted plaster, furniture, and ceramics which reveal that the tomb workers copied in modest materials for their own homes the forms they created in precious materials for the tombs of the kings and queens.

Sennedjem, the chief artist, lived in the corner house of the village just below where he built a tomb for himself, his wife, and their family members. The interior of this workman's tomb was decorated in a private version of the elaborate painted reliefs begun by the workers of Deir el-Medina for each pharaoh on his accession. The east wall of its curved-ceilinged burial chamber is decorated with a vision of the afterlife that shows Sennedjem and his wife, Iyneferti, in the Fields of Iaru, the abode of the dead who are blessed. The lunette at top shows baboons adoring the bark of the sun god, Re. Below, the waters of a great canal flow around an orchard of sycamore, doum, and date palms. Above the orchard, the couple plow, sow, and reap their grain harvest. On the opposite wall, two Anubis jackals flank an offering table. Below, Sennedjem and Iyneferti, beautifully dressed in fine white linen clothes, adore the guardians of the gates to the underworld. On the curved ceiling, Sennedjem and

Fig. 33

Fig. 40

Fig. 34

Fig. 35

Fig. 42

Fig. 41

Fig. 43

Iyneferti kneel, accepting a bounty of water and bread from a tree-spirit rising from a fruitful sycamore-fig tree. Cones of perfumed fat decorate their elaborately groomed hair. On the side wall, the mummy of Sennedjem is laid out on a grand lion bed, watched over by the guardians of the dead, Isis and Nephthys. At the funerary banquet, Sennedjem, his wife, and relatives receive offerings of flowers from their children.

Fig. 44

Fig. 46

Sennedjem's tomb is typical of New Kingdom private tombs, which include mortuary scenes such as the passage of the dead through the gates of the afterworld in addition to the agricultural, craft, and offering scenes familiar from Old Kingdom tombs. In a tomb built for Nekhtamun, head of the altar in the mortuary temple of Ramesses II, one wall displays the familiar scene of butchering to prepare an offering. Below, seated singers and a lutist entertain at the funerary banquet, to which the sons and colleagues of the deceased bring garlands and bouquets of flowers.

Fig. 38

Private tombs reflected the belief that their owners would enjoy in the afterlife a prosperous and idealized version of their mortal experience. Royal tombs were meant to help ensure the ascension of the ruler to the realm of the gods, and so their decoration was more exclusively devoted to scenes of the deceased with the gods and representations from the mortuary books that developed from the Pyramid and Coffin Texts of earlier periods. The underworld (Duat) was thought of as having twelve divisions, parallel to the twelve hours of the night. The "Book of the Underworld" and the "Book of the Gates" present these divisions through which the sun god travels accompanied by the deceased. The gate to each division is guarded by great snakes, whose names must be known for the dead to pass through. At the entrance to some tombs was inscribed the "Litany of Re," a hymn of praise to the sun god that gives his seventy-five names. Scenes of daily life were not represented because the separate mortuary temples built for each pharaoh provided for the rituals and offerings that gave sustenance to the deified ruler.

Fig. 48

Fig. 49

Thutmose III came to sole power after the death of Hatshepsut, which he may have caused. At some point later in his reign he erased her memory by usurping her inscriptions and monuments. More significantly, he enlarged Egypt's political goals beyond the stability and commercial emphasis of Hatshepsut's reign to an energetic militarism.

Thutmose III undertook regular campaigns into Palestine and Syria as far as the Euphrates River, which formed the limit of Egyptian control. In the south, he extended Egyptian power to the Fourth Cataract. Under his successors, Egypt forged alliances with the other great kingdoms of Asia Minor and the Near East, and these were sealed with royal intermarriages and hostages.

Great building projects were carried out in the Eighteenth Dynasty. A festival shrine, obelisks, and a pylon were added to the precinct of Amun, on the east bank of the Nile at Thebes. Construction also began on the Luxor Temple, dedicated to the Theban deities, Amun, his consort Mut, and their offspring, the moon god, Khons. At this temple, now in the center of the modern town of Luxor, a shrine to the three deities was built with red granite column shafts in the form of clustered papyrus stalks and bud-shaped capitals. A colonnade of immense columns with flowering papyrus capitals opened on a courtyard beyond which was built a columned vestibule that led to the sanctuary.

Fig. 50

Fig. 55

Fig. 56
Fig. 51

While royal power was strong and secure in the Eighteenth Dynasty, internal challenges to the absolute position of the pharaoh were developing in the priesthood, especially among the priests of Amun. The endowment of fields, cattle, timber, slaves, gold, and gems to support temple rituals had, over centuries, centralized great economic power in the hands of the priests. The wealth generated by the temple estates is reflected in the tomb of Neferronpet, who was also called Kenro, a scribe in the treasury of Amun-Re responsible for keeping the accounts of the craftsmen of the treasury. In the lively paintings of his tomb, a harpist serenades as Kenro balances a knucklebone playing a board game, tilted up to show its top surface. Kenro and his wife, Mutemwia, are shown dressed in luxurious linen robes sitting in an arbor resting their feet on papyrus mats. Under her stool, a cat gnaws at a bone. Kenro's rank is displayed by the scepter he holds up in his left hand. Smaller figures fill the other walls of this tomb. Kenro is shown seated, watching the weighing of gold, while farther along workers carry goods into the great treasury of Amun. The rectangular doorway of each of these many strongrooms is shown flat against the wall surface.

Fig. 39

Fig. 36

To control the power that devolved from such wealth, and possibly from a personal conviction in sun cult beliefs that had a long history in Egypt and also existed elsewhere in the Middle East, the tenth pharaoh of the Eighteenth Dynasty, Amenhotep IV, removed the capital from Thebes to Middle Egypt. There, at Amarna, he founded a new city with a palace and built a great temple to a single solar deity, the sun-disc, Aten. During the reign of this pharaoh, who took a new name, Akhenaten, concern with religious reform took precedence over political administration, and there was little interest in controlling the territories into which Egypt had expanded in the early phases of the dynasty. Egypt's foreign empire began to collapse, a process that was not remedied during the brief reign of the following pharaoh, the young Prince Tutankhamen, famed in our time because of the splendor of his burial.

At the end of the Eighteenth Dynasty, control of the country was taken over by a powerful military leader, Horemheb. The instability that had accompanied the short reigns of Akhenaten's successors made the reestablishment of orderly government and of religious institutions of highest priority. Once accomplished under Horemheb, Egypt's energy and resources were again directed at expansion in the northeast by military and political means.

A general, Ramesses I, was selected as successor by the childless Horemheb to be the founder of the Nineteenth Dynasty. He was especially well suited to begin the efforts to reassert Egyptian power in the Near East. His family originated in a town of the northeast Delta, Tanis, which provided him first-hand knowledge of and interest in the Egyptian garrisons beyond the frontier, across the Sinai in Palestine and Syria. Ramesses I had risen through various military positions to serve as vizier, chief deputy of the pharaoh, and was therefore privy to diplomatic and administrative affairs. He was not young when he became pharaoh, and enjoyed only a sixteen-month rule before his death.

The Nineteenth Dynasty pharaohs followed the tradition established in the preceding dynasty of constructing mortuary temples at the edge of the agricultural zone on the west bank of the Nile across from Thebes and separate tombs in the Valley of the Kings in the desert ravines hidden away in the hills beyond. The Tomb of Ramesses I, needed unexpectedly soon, consisted only of two steep stairs, a corridor, and an unfinished antechamber before the burial chamber. The walls were plastered and painted in the same technique that had been used in the tomb of Horemheb. The decision to use this process may have been influenced by the fact that

there had not been time for the long process of cutting the scenes in relief. Its walls carry large images of Ramesses with the gods, and smaller scenes illustrating passages from the Book of Gates. As no separate funerary temple had been built, the funerary cult of Ramesses I was conducted in a sanctuary within the mortuary temple built by his son and successor.

Fig. 24

The new pharaoh, Sety I, began a campaign of expansion along the Mediterranean coast of Palestine up to Lebanon. In this period, political control over the coastal plain was exercised by the strongest power among the Hittites of the Anatolian plateau (now central Turkey), Egypt, and the various powers of the Mesopotamian basin, including the Mitanni. Trade and military movements were controlled by strongholds along the roadway through Gaza and by domination of the towns of the inland valley, Beit Shean, Megiddo, and Kadesh.

Fig. 63

These campaigns were commemorated on the walls of a great hall of columns begun under Sety I at the Temple of Amun at Karnak, a structure that would be completed under his son and successor, Ramesses II. Its interior walls were decorated with reliefs showing these pharaohs honoring the traditional gods of Thebes in scenes of offerings. The reliefs covering the exterior walls commemorate the great battles of Sety I and Ramesses II. On a short section of the northeast exterior wall, dwellers of Canaan are shown begging Sety I for mercy before their fortified city. Below, a great Sety in his war chariot takes aim at the dwellers of Palestine, whose dead are heaped up beneath the plunging feet of his plumed horses. At the top right of the lower register of this relief, the protective wings of the vulture of Upper Egypt protect the king in battle.

North of Palestine, the Beka'a Valley runs roughly parallel to the eastern Mediterranean coast, but is shielded from the sea by a range of low, coastal mountains, the source in antiquity of famed cedar lumber. To the east the valley is bordered by the anti-Lebanon, a second range that protects it from the deserts of eastern Syria. The Beka'a Valley, about ten miles wide and eighty miles long, is drained to the south by the Litani River and to the north by the Orontes. It provided the only inland north-south route in this region, and whoever controlled it was able also to command the trade route access to the Mediterranean ports. In antiquity, as now, it has been the focus of conflict in the Near East.

In the Ramesside period, its major settlement, key to the sovereignty of a wide area, was Kadesh, a fortified hill on the Orontes River where the Beka'a Valley opens into the river plain. The boundary between Hittite and Egyptian spheres of influence was established at the Orontes through battle and diplomatic agreement. Beginning in the first summer of his rule, Sety I led Egyptian forces as far north, probably, as Tyre. In the following summer campaigns he secured Egyptian hegemony as far as Damascus. Hittite strength prevented an indefinite expansion as did the logistical problems of an overly extended supply route; therefore, although under Sety I the Egyptian army did take Kadesh, its hold over the fort had to be relinquished. A young participant in the Egyptian victory, Ramesses II, would renew the attempt to control inland Syria.

Sety I guarded his throne against usurpation by designating Ramesses II as his successor, and, although still an adolescent, he was accorded the insignia, crown, and household establishment of a ruler. In these years of peace, a number of extraordinary building projects were under way. At the ancient religious center of Abydos, a temple to Osiris, the gods of Egypt, and the ruler was built and decorated with fine painted reliefs. At Abydos is inscribed a list naming the pharaohs who had reigned over Egypt, preserving the sequence—minus the names of Hatshepsut and the Amarna kings—for history. Across the Nile from Thebes, the funerary temple and the large, elaborately decorated tomb of Sety I were also being built. When the pharaoh died in the sixteenth year of his rule, he was buried in this tomb that had five corridors and descending steps connecting five rooms that led to the burial chamber. In place of the stars often used to decorate ceilings in temples and tombs, its curved roof carries an astronomical scene. Some of the constellations illustrated, like the lion and bull, we find familiar, but others, the crocodile, hippopotamus, and hawk, are denizens of a different mythological world.

Fig. 27

The mortuary rites of Sety I were performed at a temple constructed at the northern end of the plain along the west bank of the river. The two courts that formed its front end have been lost to erosion, but the colonnade of the west side of the court and portions of the beautifully decorated shrines within are preserved. Past the colonnade is the hypostyle hall, its ceiling still in place with its decoration of winged solar disk, vultures, and cartouches of Sety I

Fig. 64

Fig. 65
Fig. 66

enclosed by snakes. Beyond are the sanctuaries, dedicated as in other royal mortuary temples to the Theban triad, Amun, Mut, and Khonsu. In a tradition that goes back to the earliest tombs of the Old Kingdom and the mortuary temples of the great pyramids, the New Kingdom funerary temples include a relief depicting a false door, the point at which the dead ruler contacts the world of the living to receive the offerings needed for eternal sustenance.

Following the death of Sety I, the sixty-six-year-long reign of Ramesses II proceeded without opposition. In the early years of his rule, his major attention was devoted to internal affairs. He reformed religious institutions and undertook the completion of building activities begun during the reign of Sety I, including his mortuary temple. Ramesses fathered many children by his queens and other women of the harem. His first wife, Queen Nefertari, appears prominently in many, although not all, sculptures of the reign. As the mother of his eldest son, for a time she played the dominant role among these women.

Fig. 58

Fig. 59

In the fifth year of his rule, Ramesses II renewed military efforts in Lebanon. This campaign was frequently recorded on reliefs and is known in considerable detail. The climactic episode occurred at Kadesh, where the Egyptian army, purposely misled by Hittite secret agents into thinking that the enemy was still distant, and with its four divisions widely dispersed, set up its camp before the town. The Hittites, waiting in ambush, defeated one division before it could come into play and attacked the Egyptian encampment. The rout was complete except for a small group under the direct control of Ramesses, which fought clear to join up with a third division as it arrived from the coast and carried out a successful counter-attack. The near devastation accorded the Egyptians made clear that further extension of their power north into Syria was not possible. The Hittite account of this battle, preserved in the archives excavated at their capital, Hattusas, considers the outcome an Egyptian defeat. The reliefs at Karnak, Luxor, Abu Simbel, and the Mortuary Temple of Ramesses II treat the battle as a great victory for Egypt. The personal heroism and leadership of Ramesses II might be considered a personal victory for the pharaoh, but the actual result was superiority for neither side. The boundary established by this battle was further recognized sixteen years later by an elaborate treaty between the Egyptians and the Hittites, regulating the relationship between

Fig. 83

the two powers. Egyptian attempts to control northern Syria carried on in the interim had not succeeded, and the documents drawn up gave recognition to the de facto stalemate. This treaty endured until the collapse of the Hittite empire, and was sealed well after its enactment by the marriage of a Hittite princess to Ramesses.

Construction activity reached a high level during the reign of Ramesses II. A prolonged period of political stability both within Egypt and in its territories abroad, combined with increased wealth, permitted an ambitious program of monumental architectural projects. The activity was stimulated in part by the personal ambition of Ramesses II and partly by his politically astute plan to express the power and authority of his position as divine ruler. The demand for skilled craftsmen so outstripped the supply of trained talent that the level of accomplishment did not uniformly reach the quality of some earlier periods. However, through the expressive use of monumental scale and the insistent repetition of a limited repertoire of themes, a powerful result was achieved. As new structures were built or others, previously started, were completed, the surfaces of their monumental gateways and sanctuary pillars and walls were decorated with stories of the pharaoh's exploits. These reliefs and inscriptions were brightly painted. Now, the color long weathered away, the relief surfaces worn down, and portions defaced or broken away, they lack the immediate clarity and narrative power of their original design. At a few sites, traces of color still project the splendor of their original appearance. One of the grandest of these barely escaped destruction just two decades ago.

When the High Dam was built just beyond Aswan in the 1960s, replacing earlier efforts to control the river, the agricultural zone along the Nile valley as far as the border with Sudan was permanently inundated. The towns in this area were moved to new settlements north of Aswan, and a program of salvage archaeology was instituted to retrieve as much information about the Nubian past as time permitted. Now, the vast expanse of Lake Nasser is set in a barren desert broken only by the rock formations that wind and erosion have created.

Fig. 68 Over 160 miles beyond Aswan, at Abu Simbel, a pair of temples was cut into the rock at a place where the face of the cliff was bowed forward in two curving bays. These rock-cut temples from the period of Ramesses II would have been permanently lost under the lake forming behind the dam. In a unique international effort, under the sponsorship of the United Nations agency, UNESCO, these temples and their sculptural decoration were cut free from the rock and reassembled nearby above the waterline. Oval domes of reinforced concrete, situated to reproduce the orientation of the original sites, were built large enough to surround the inner chambers of the temples. Just as in ancient times, twice each year, at the spring and autumn equinoxes, the rising sun penetrates into the sanctuary to illuminate the images deep within. A modern feat of international cooperation and engineering skill has preserved these sanctuaries in a dramatic setting along the edge of the lake.

The larger of the temples is dedicated to Ramesses II and Re of Heliopolis as Re-Herakhty. Two principal gods of Egypt, Amun, the god of Thebes, and Ptah, the creator god of Memphis, were also venerated and represented in the innermost shrine. On a terrace before the facade, four seated colossi of Ramesses II flank the entrance. Three smaller sculptures representing members of the family of Ramesses stand against the lower legs of each colossus, with Queen Nefertari, shown three times, given prominence. Small images of the falcon Horus and Ramesses are lined up at the edge of the parapet before the feet of the colossal facade sculptures. Over the portal is an image of Re-Herakhty, holding in his hands the jackal-headed staff, the *user*, and the hieroglyph for justice, *maat*, forming with the god Re a rebus for the throne name of Ramesses II, *User-Maat-Re*. Images of Ramesses adoring Re-Herakhty and his deified self are cut in relief to either side. Below, flanking the entranceway, the sides of the thrones are decorated with the unification relief, the Nile gods binding Upper and Lower Egypt. Beneath are reliefs of the defeated enemies of Egypt, those of the North, Syrians, on the north side and on the south side the enemies of the South, Nubians. Each morning, the rising sun floods over the facade from the top down, first lighting up the row of baboons, adorants of the sun, that surmount the facade.

The interior reliefs are extraordinarily well preserved because of the isolated location of the temples and the protection of their cave-like setting. The story of the battle at Kadesh is illustrated again, with striking narrative detail. On the inner face of the entrance wall to the right of the entrance door, Ramesses II is shown striding forward in the traditional pose of conquest, his hand grasping a clump of

Fig. 69
Fig. 70

Fig. 73

Fig. 76

Fig. 72

Fig. 67

Fig. 81

Fig. 80

defeated enemies. At the center of the clump of heads is a single face represented frontally, a rare occurrence in Egyptian art that was reserved almost exclusively for this compositional type. Images of Ramesses in the pose of Osiris flank the main aisle. Across the rear of the sanctuary, deep within the cave-like interior, is an image of Ramesses seated in the company of the great gods Ptah, Amun-Re, and Re-Herakhty, an equal divinity with the supreme gods of the land.

Fig. 79

A smaller temple was built lower down and about four hundred feet to the north, its facade rising just above water level. It is dedicated to the deified queen of Ramesses II, Nefertari, and the goddess Hathor. Colossal standing figures of Ramesses and Nefertari as Hathor, separated by sloping buttresses, flank the doorway. Pillars in the interior are decorated with a sistrum, a ceremonial rattle associated with Hathor, and the cow-eared Hathor and images of Ramesses, Nefertari, and other deities. Beyond this hall and a transverse vestibule lies the sanctuary, a shrine in its rear wall decorated with a relief of Ramesses under the protection of Hathor.

Fig. 71

Some mortuary temples built on the west bank across from Thebes have been obliterated by flooding and erosion. The Colossi of Memnon, two enormous seated figures of Amenhotep III, stand marooned in a lush field, the temple they fronted now totally lost. We are fortunate that the Funerary Temple of Ramesses II, slightly farther south along the edge of the agricultural plain, has suffered much less, because few sights from ancient or modern times arouse as intense a response as the remains of this great ruin, the Ramesseum. In its first court lies the tumbled torso of an immense colossus that once fronted its second pylon. Its great height of almost sixty feet is now reduced to an imposing ruin, a sobering reminder of the transitory frailty of human existence. Shelley's sonnet *Ozymandias*, its name drawn from the Greek transliteration of *User-Maat-Re*, the throne name of Ramesses II, inspired by the wrecked colossus of the Ramesseum, captures this reflective mood.

Fig. 85

> I met a traveller from an antique land
> Who said: Two vast and trunkless legs of stone
> Stand in the desert. Near them on the sand,
> Half sunk, a shatter'd visage lies, whose frown
> And wrinkled lip and sneer of cold command

> Tell that its sculptor well those passions read
> Which yet survive, stamp'd on these lifeless things,
> The hand that mock'd them, and the heart that fed;
> And on the pedestal these words appear:
> 'My name is Ozymandias, king of kings:
> Look on my works, ye Mighty, and despair!'
> Nothing beside remains. Round the decay
> Of that colossal wreck, boundless and bare,
> The lone and level sands stretch far away.

Beyond lies a fine granite head of Ramesses, fallen to the ground in the second court, a fragment of the two granite colossi that flanked the steps leading up into the hall of columns and the sanctuary.

Fig. 84

The plan of the Ramesseum includes a small palace placed at a right angle to the south side of the first court. It provided a stopping place for the pharaoh and his retinue during visits to the west bank of the Nile, across the river from Thebes. The temple proper is surrounded on the north, west, and south sides by parallel rows of vaulted storage rooms built of mud brick. These great storerooms of grain protected Egypt in times of drought. The use of arch construction, already found at the Mortuary Temple of Hatshepsut, was reserved for subsidiary and functional structures such as storerooms. Ancient Egyptian architecture is of post-and-lintel construction, vertical uprights supporting horizontal beams. The dynamic energy of weight and support in vaulted construction was clearly felt unsuitable to Egyptian religious and funerary belief.

In the ruins of the Ramesseum we find recapitulated the expressive power achieved in the Nineteenth Dynasty through immense scale and the repetition of decorative elements in relief and sculpture in the round. The pylon reliefs publicized imperial rule beyond the boundaries of Egypt and commemorated the heroic actions of the pharaoh. Decipherment of the reliefs, even where fragmentary, is possible because the primary theme, the battle of Kadesh, was represented repeatedly at different locations, and missing sections can be interpolated. Egyptian soldiers, lined up behind their protective armament of shields, march implacably to war in Syria. Shown hugely larger than his allies or opponents, the great Ramesses II rushes on his chariot into battle, throwing the Hittites into tumbled disarray and defeat. The Orontes River sweeps around rows of Hittite

Fig. 82

Fig. 89

Fig. 86
Fig. 88
Fig. 87

soldiers, lined up behind other troops already fallen into chaos and defeat. Farther within the temple, images of Ramesses in the form of the god of the underworld, Osiris, line the front and rear of the second court. The hypostyle hall follows, its central aisle flanked by papyrus flower capitals, its side aisles by papyrus bud capitals.

Fig. 90

Fig. 92

The last great funerary temple of the Ramesside period, farther south along the west bank of the Nile across from Thebes at Medinet Habu, was built as the Mortuary Temple of Ramesses III, son of the usurper Setnakht, founder of the Twentieth Dynasty. Here the modern tourist experiences very strikingly the original spatial experience and colorful decoration of monumental Egyptian architecture. Palace, funerary shrine, and later fortress, this great construction closely followed the design of the Ramesseum. A towered gate through an enormously tall enclosure wall gave entrance to the temple and subsidiary storerooms. The palace projected south from the first court. The upper floors of the gateway are preserved, including the relief-covered walls of its upper rooms. These scenes show the pharaoh and women of the harem at rest, as they might have visited these rooms to enjoy the view over the green fields stretching east toward the Nile, closer then than now. This construction was not impregnable, but its imposing architecture provided a sense of security to the local population and invincibility to any potential invaders, a reflection of the increased instability of the Twentieth Dynasty.

Fig. 91
Fig. 93

The southwest colonnade inside the first court formed the entrance facade for the royal palace built outward from the side of the temple. A projecting bay in the center of the wall behind these columns is pierced by a "Window of Appearance" where the pharaoh could appear to the people and bestow gifts and honors. A projecting corbel decorated with the heads of enemies protrudes from this bay just below scenes of the pharaoh triumphing over Egypt's enemies. Doorways on either side of the bay gave entrance to the palace during the Festival of Opet and the Festival of the Valley, when images of the gods were brought over to the west bank from Thebes.

Egypt was not immune to the convulsive waves of immigration that brought conflict leading to profound political and social change to the Near East at the end of the second millennium B.C., among them the fall of Troy. The reliefs at Medinet Habu are of great historical interest to the under-

standing of this period. They represent various ethnic groups of the Middle East and the Aegean at war with the Egyptians. The first pylon shows Ramesses III triumphing over the Libyans. A long inscription on the right side of the gateway records the victory. Reliefs on the exterior of the temple wall show Egyptians at war with Libyans, with peoples from Palestine, and with the People of the Sea, a sea-going group of foreigners. Scenes of these last people on the march with carts of possessions and their families may reflect these times of immigration and chaos.

Fig. 95

Beyond the eleventh century B.C. and the end of the New Kingdom, rule over Egypt shifted among internal and external powers. Descendants of Libyan mercenaries controlled the monarchy of the Twenty-second and Twenty-third dynasties. Kushites from the south invaded Egypt in the eighth century B.C. and controlled it until expelled early in the seventh century by the Assyrians. After a period of native rule and cultural vitality under the Twenty-sixth (Saite) Dynasty, the Persians ruled from the last quarter of the sixth century to the late fifth century B.C., and again in the fourth century. But in 332 B.C. Egypt, along with the rest of the Middle East, fell to the armies of Alexander the Great. In the succeeding three hundred years and the following period of Roman rule, Egyptian religious and cultural life proceeded with a veneer of classical culture that had only limited impact on the indigenous traditions of religious belief and architectural and artistic production. The new city established on the Mediterranean coast, at the site of modern Alexandria, represented an outpost of Hellenized culture that had little effect on the ancient traditions in Upper Egypt. The temples built during the Ptolemaic and Roman periods in Upper Egypt are Egyptian in character, and demonstrate the essential features of Egyptian religious architecture and sculpture with only limited influence from non-Egyptian sources.

The site of Edfu, located about halfway between Luxor and Aswan, had been a religious center since much earlier times, as the location of one of the great battles between Horus and Seth. A temple was built between 237 and 57 B.C., during the Ptolemaic period, dedicated to Horus, his consort, Hathor, and their son. Additions continued, as at many major temples, in the Roman period. Its excellent state of preservation, including the interior stairs and roofing slabs, allows the modern visitor to experience the

Fig. 102

dramatic sequence of vertical pylon, brilliantly lit open courtyard, and progressively darker halls leading to the sanctuary, deep inside. Two great granite falcons, images of Horus, flank the pylon entrance. A high enclosure wall surrounding the entire temple was decorated on its inner face with scenes from the battle of Horus and Seth and other religious motifs.

A second of the major temples of this late period was built at Kom Ombo, the center of a fertile plain at a crossroads where the north-south route through Upper Egypt to Nubia meets a major road through the desert to the east. Today, the plain is mainly planted in sugar cane, and a large refinery dominates the town, still a major trading center. When approached from the Nile, the preserved portion of the temple at Kom Ombo lies exposed in cross section, its front end partially carried away by the river's erosion. The rich floral capitals of the vestibule behind its open court

Fig. 99

now stand clearly visible on the crest of the temple hill above the modern embankment. The temple was dedicated to both the crocodile-headed god Sobek and the falcon-headed Haroeris, the elder Horus, their consorts and offspring. Crocodiles had been venerated at Kom Ombo from a much earlier period, and a small pool may have been used for raising baby crocodiles to be mummified and given by pilgrims as votive offerings. A sample of these crocodiles, originally entombed in crypts beneath the temple's twin sanctuaries, is now displayed in a subsidiary shrine to the south of the temple court.

The Kom Ombo Temple was built in the reign of Ptolemy VI Philometor (181–146 B.C.). During the Hellenistic period, Egypt enjoyed a renewed prosperity under the rule of the Ptolemaic kings, descendants of a Macedonian Greek general from the army of Alexander the Great. The temple at Kom Ombo drew pilgrims seeking healing, and their games, inscriptions, incised ships and outlines of the feet they scratched into the pavement are still visible.

The decoration of the temple continued well into the succeeding Roman period, but the content and basic stylistic approach of the reliefs clearly follows the established Egyptian tradition. The surviving lower courses of the entrance pylon carry a series of offering bearers, bringing

Fig. 100

gifts of animals, birds, and precious oils to the gods of Ombos. The bottom of all of the vestibule columns proclaim a hymn of adoration through their scenes of pinioned

lapwings, *rekhyt* birds, and stars rising from papyrus clusters, the hieroglyphic message meaning "all mankind adores." The temple's reliefs show Ptolemaic rulers and queens before the gods and goddesses venerated here. In one panel, Ptolemy VI is approached by a trio of the temple's deities, the crocodile god, Sobek, the falcon-headed elder Horus, Haroeris, and the moon god, Khons, who writes on a palm rib. The king, Sobek, and Haroeris each clutch an *ankh*, the symbol of life. Bull's tails, part of traditional regalia from at least the First Dynasty on, symbolize the power of the gods. The soft, rounded modeling of the figures, typical of Ptolemaic relief style, lends a fleshy appearance to these powerful images. Beyond a narrow passageway, a high enclosure wall encircles the temple, protecting the reliefs of the Roman period carried on its outer walls. On the temple's east face, a lion crouches at the sandalled foot of the emperor, devouring the extended arms of a clump of Egypt's enemies. Its powerful claws rake the repeated shapes of their buttocks and feet. This smiting scene follows a tradition as old as the earliest representations of Egypt's pharaohs, in an unbroken series of examples extending for over three thousand years.

Fig. 98

Fig. 96

Fig. 97

From the unification of Egypt near the close of the fourth millennium B.C. to the last stages of Roman rule over Egypt more than three thousand years later, Egypt's prosperity depended on the military power, administrative skill, and diplomatic wisdom of its ruler. At every stage, lacking this, the country was vulnerable to invasion and chaos. Yet essential features persisted and developed over these many centuries. Egyptian culture assimilated only limited aspects of other religious and social constructs as an overlay of the embedded tradition. By the late Roman period, however, Egypt faced its first radical transformation when the Roman world became Christianized. By the time of the Arab conquest in 640 A.D., the country more thoroughly turned away from the last vestiges of its ancient beliefs. In its turn, Arab Egypt may very well live as long as pharaonic Egypt, the major link between these ages being the cultural persistence that has let Egypt endure challenges and developments without a complete overthrow of its religious, artistic, and social customs. Guided through the alien world of its more distant past by its knowledgeable guardians of today, we meet grandeur and mystery whose power has endured from the earliest stages of human history.

Plates

1. Pyramids of Cheops (left) and Chephren, Giza.

2. West hall, Temple of Ptah, Memphis.

3. Desert cliffs of West Thebes across the Nile at sunrise, Luxor.

4. West hall, Temple of Ptah, Memphis.

5. *Ahmed Khalifa at Temple of Amun at Karnak, Thebes.*

6. Entrance through enclosure wall, funerary precinct of Djoser, Saqqara.

7. Entrance colonnade, funerary precinct of Djoser, Saqqara.

8. House of the South (?), funerary precinct of Djoser, Saqqara.

9. Pyramids of Chephren (rear), Mycerinus, and Queens of Mycerinus from the southwest, Giza.

10. Enclosure wall and Step Pyramid, funerary precinct of Djoser, Saqqara.

11. Sphinx, funerary complex of Chephren, Giza.

12. Inscription from mastaba of Khenu, Saqqara.

1 3. Restoration inscription on rock wall parallel to north face of Pyramid of Chephren with Pyramid of Cheops (rear), Giza.

14. Gateway to mortuary temple, Pyramid of Unas, Saqqara.

15. Tomb chamber, Pyramid of Unas, Saqqara.

16. *Pharaoh Ramesses II receiving ankh (life) from Re, second court, Funerary Temple of Ramesses III at Medinet Habu, West Thebes.*

17. Thoth, the ibis-headed patron of scribes and god of wisdom (center), flanked by scenes of Pharaoh Ramesses II led into the temple by
Atum and the war god, Month (center left), and kneeling before the Theban triad of Amun, Mut, and Khuns (center right),
south exterior entrance wall of hypostyle hall, Funerary Temple of Ramesses II (Ramesseum), West Thebes.

18. Pharaoh Ramesses I (right) offering wine to Nefertum, with tyet at left, Tomb of Ramesses I (Tomb 16), Valley of the Kings, West Thebes.

19. Pharaoh Ramesses I (center left) before Ptah, flanked by Maat, goddess of Truth (left) and djed (right), Tomb of Ramesses I (Tomb 16), Valley of the Kings, West Thebes.

20. Pharaoh Merenptah (left) before Re-Herakhty, Tomb of Merenptah (Tomb 8), Valley of the Kings, West Thebes.

21. Hathor head (interior pillar) and Nefertari offering flowers (left foreground), Temple of Nefertari, Abu Simbel.

22. *Osiris before an offering table flanked by protective eyes* (wedjat) *and animal skin fetishes* (ut), *Tomb of Sennedjem* (*Tomb 1*), *Deir el-Medina, West Thebes.*

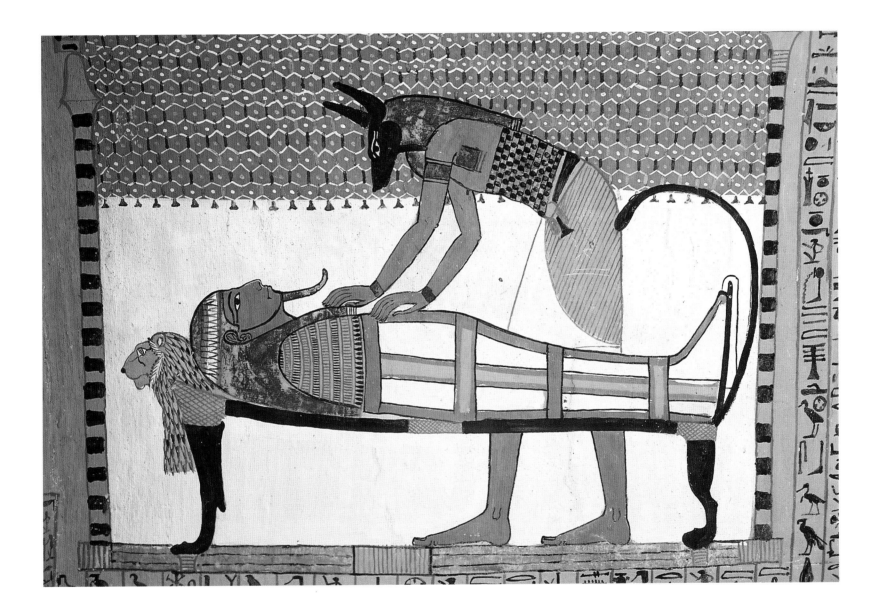

23. *Anubis, guardian of the necropolis, preparing mummy, Tomb of Sennedjem (Tomb 1), Deir el-Medina, West Thebes.*

24. *Pharaoh Ramesses I guided by Anubis (right) and Harsiesi (Horus), Tomb of Ramesses I (Tomb 16), Valley of the Kings, West Thebes.*

25. Black granite statue of Sekhmet, Funerary Temple of Ramesses III at Medinet Habu, West Thebes.

26. Isis, Tomb of Sety I (Tomb 17), Valley of the Kings, West Thebes.

27. *Constellations, ceiling of burial chamber, Tomb of Sety I (Tomb 17), Valley of the Kings, West Thebes.*

28. *A funerary bark passing through the divisions of the underworld bearing a scarab, Tomb of Sety I (Tomb 17),*
Valley of the Kings, West Thebes.

29. Divine cow supported by Shu, the god of air, and other deities, Tomb of Sety I (Tomb 17), Valley of the Kings, West Thebes.

30. Columns in hypostyle hall, Temple of Amun at Karnak, Thebes.

31. *Ram-headed sphinxes of Amun protecting Pharaoh Ramesses II, Temple of Amun at Karnak, Thebes.*

32. Relief of Pharaoh offering, Temple of Amun at Karnak, Thebes.

33. Funerary Temple of Queen Hatshepsut, Deir el-Bahari, West Thebes.

34. House remains and principal street of tomb workers' village, Deir el-Medina, West Thebes.

35. Craftsmen making burial furnishings, Tomb of sculptor Ipuy (Tomb 217), West Thebes.

36. Workmen pile up offerings in treasuries of Temple of Amun at Karnak,
and Neferronpet (Kenro) supervises weighing of gold (lower right), Tomb of Neferronpet (Tomb 178), West Thebes.

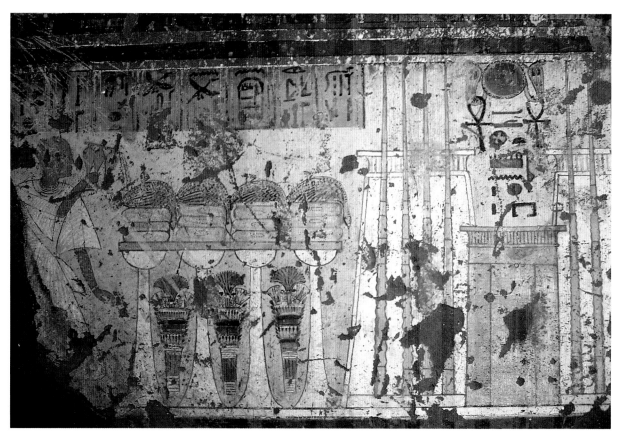

37. Offering tables before temple pylon, Tomb of Panehesi (Tomb 16), West Thebes.

38. *Animal butchering and procession of offering bearers, Tomb of Nekhtamun (Tomb 341), West Thebes.*

39. *Blind harpist entertaining at the funerary banquet of Neferronpet (Kenro) and his wife who play a board game in a pavilion (left),*
Tomb of Neferronpet (Tomb 178), West Thebes.

40. Entrance, Tomb of Paser (Tomb 106), West Thebes.

41. *Baboons adoring Re, Tomb of Sennedjem (Tomb 1), Deir el-Medina, West Thebes.*

42. Baboons adoring Re, funerary rites, and fields of Iaru, Tomb of Sennedjem (Tomb 1), Deir el-Medina, West Thebes.

43. *Sennedjem and wife adoring gods of the underworld, Tomb of Sennedjem (Tomb 1), Deir el-Medina, West Thebes.*

44. *Goddess appearing in a tree before Sennedjem and his wife, ceiling, Tomb of Sennedjem (Tomb 1), Deir el-Medina, West Thebes.*

45. *Sennedjem plowing and wife sowing, Tomb of Sennedjem (Tomb 1), Deir el-Medina, West Thebes.*

46. Guests at the funerary banquet receive offerings, above them the mummy of Sennedjem guarded by Isis and Nephthys in the shape of hawks, Tomb of Sennedjem (Tomb 1), Deir el-Medina, West Thebes.

47. Sennedjem and his wife before the knife-wielding Guardians of the Gates of the Underworld; below are relatives at the funerary banquet, Tomb of Sennedjem (Tomb 1), Deir el-Medina, West Thebes.

48. *Within a shrine, ram-headed Re passes by boat through a division of the snake-guarded Underworld, Tomb of Ramesses I (Tomb 16),*
Valley of the Kings, West Thebes.

49. Inside the tomb entrance, the Litany of Re inscription flanks a sun disc bearing the ram-headed Re and a scarab, a crocodile (below), snake, and a cow, Tomb of Ramesses II (Tomb 7), Valley of the Kings, West Thebes.

50. Obelisk of Thutmose I viewed from hypostyle hall, Temple of Amun at Karnak, Thebes.

51. Columns in forecourt of Amenhotep III, Temple of Amun, Mut, and Khons, Luxor.

52. Procession to Karnak during Festival of Opet, inner face, west side of enclosure wall of processional colonnade, Temple of Amun, Mut, and Khons, Luxor.

53. Colossus of Pharaoh Ramesses II and bottom of obelisk with baboons adoring the sun, before entrance pylon, Temple of Amun, Mut, and Khons, Luxor.

54. *View through entrance to processional colonnade, Temple of Amun, Mut, and Khons, Luxor.*

55. Granite shrine in forecourt, Temple of Amun, Mut, and Khons, Luxor.

56. *View north through processional colonnade, Temple of Amun, Mut, and Khons, Luxor.*

57. Papyrus cluster columns, Court of Amenhotep III, Temple of Amun, Mut, and Khons, Luxor.

58. Pharaoh Ramesses II, *forecourt, Temple of Amun, Mut, and Khons, Luxor.*

59. Nefertari by leg of Ramesses II, forecourt, Temple of Amun, Mut, and Khons, Luxor.

60. Columns in hypostyle hall, Temple of Amun at Karnak, Thebes.

61. Statue base inscribed with cartouches of Pharaoh Ramesses II, Temple of Amun, Mut, and Khons, Luxor.

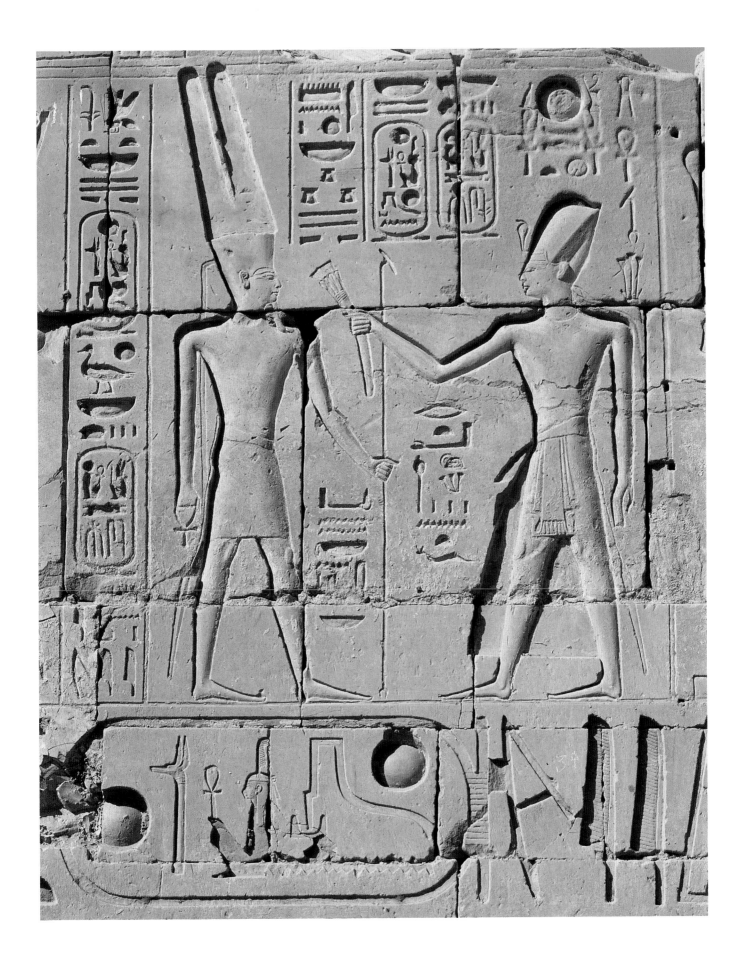

62. Pharaoh Ramesses II (right) offering flowers to Amun, Temple of Amun at Karnak, Thebes.

63. Sety I in Palestine conquers Bedouin (below) and is begged for mercy by inhabitants of Canaanite fortress (above), northeast exterior wall of hypostyle hall, Temple of Amun at Karnak, Thebes.

64. Papyrus cluster columns in forecourt form entrance colonnade, Funerary Temple of Sety I, West Thebes.

65. *Winged solar disk, flying vultures, and the names of Sety I flanked by snakes, ceiling of hypostyle hall, Funerary Temple of Sety I, West Thebes.*

66. *View up to transverse hall from hypostyle hall, Funerary Temple of Sety I, West Thebes.*

67. Union of Egypt represented by the gods of Upper and Lower Egypt binding together with lotus and papyrus a windpipe and lungs, the hieroglyphic sign meaning "unite," entranceway, Temple of Ramesses II, Abu Simbel.

68. Colossal statue of Ramesses II, Abu Simbel.

69. South side of facade in afternoon light, Temple of Ramesses II, Abu Simbel.

70. North side of facade in afternoon light, Temple of Ramesses II, Abu Simbel.

71. Facade, Temple of Nefertari, Abu Simbel.

72. Re-Herakhty, wall above entrance, Temple of Ramesses II, Abu Simbel.

73. Nefertari next to Ramesses II, north side of entranceway, Temple of Ramesses II, Abu Simbel.

74. Horus falcons at edge of parapet, facade, Temple of Ramesses II, Abu Simbel.

75. Horus falcon at edge of parapet, facade, Temple of Ramesses II, Abu Simbel.

76. Colossi of Ramesses II, north side of facade, Temple of Ramesses II, Abu Simbel.

77. Head of Ramesses II at south end of entrance facade, Temple of Ramesses II, Abu Simbel.

78. Images of Ramesses II as Osiris flank the central aisle leading to the sanctuary (rear), Temple of Ramesses II, Abu Simbel.

79. Ramesses II as Osiris, central aisle of main hall, Temple of Ramesses II, Abu Simbel.

80. *Ramesses II defeating enemies, interior of entrance wall, north side, Temple of Ramesses II, Abu Simbel.*

81. Enemies from the north bound with papyrus, north side of entranceway, Temple of Ramesses II, Abu Simbel.

82. *Egyptian soldiers holding body shields in formation, first pylon, west face of north tower, Funerary Temple of Ramesses II (Ramesseum),*
West Thebes.

83. Battle of Kadesh along Orontes River (upper right), second pylon, west face of south tower, Funerary Temple of Ramesses II (Ramesseum), West Thebes.

84. Head of Ramesses II, second court, Funerary Temple of Ramesses II (Ramesseum), West Thebes.

85. *Fragments of granite colossus, first court, Funerary Temple of Ramesses II (Ramesseum), West Thebes.*

86. Statues of Ramesses II as Osiris line west side of second court, Funerary Temple of Ramesses II (Ramesseum), West Thebes.

87. Ramesses II in chariot attacking Hittites, Battle of Kadesh, *second pylon, west face of north tower*, Funerary Temple of Ramesses II (Ramesseum), *West Thebes*.

88. Columns with papyrus calyx capitals flank central aisle of hypostyle hall, Funerary Temple of Ramesses II (Ramesseum), *West Thebes*

89. Side aisle columns with papyrus bud capitals, hypostyle hall, Funerary Temple of Ramesses II (Ramesseum), West Thebes.

90. *View through second pylon of Funerary Temple of Ramesses III at Medinet Habu, West Thebes.*

91. South wall of first court with Pharaoh's *"Window of Appearances"* partly visible at right of center column, Funerary Temple of Ramesses III at Medinet Habu, West Thebes.

92. Protective wings of the vulture goddess of Upper Egypt, Nekhbet, decorate lintels and ceiling between second court and hypostyle hall, Funerary Temple of Ramesses III at Medinet Habu, West Thebes.

93. Colonnade before entrance wall of palace, south side of first court, Funerary Temple of Ramesses III at Medinet Habu, West Thebes.

94. Capital supporting architraves, second court, Funerary Temple of Ramesses III at Medinet Habu, *West Thebes.*

95. Pharaoh smiting the enemies of Egypt, enclosure wall, Funerary Temple of Ramesses III at Medinet Habu, West Thebes.

96. Ptolemy VI Philometor (left) approached by Hor Khonsu writing on palm rib, Haroeris (the elder Horus), and crocodile-headed Sobek, entrance to the two sanctuaries, Temple of Sobek and Haroeris, Kom Ombo.

97. Lion devouring a cluster of the enemies of Egypt, outer surface of exterior wall, east side, Temple of Sobek and Haroeris, Kom Ombo.

98. Hieroglyphic inscriptions on the hypostyle hall columns proclaim *"All mankind adores,"* Temple of Sobek and Haroeris, Kom Ombo.

99. *Variegated floral capitals, hypostyle hall, Temple of Sobek and Haroeris, Kom Ombo.*

100. *Offering bearers, exterior of entrance pylon, Temple of Sobek and Haroeris, Kom Ombo.*

101. Hieroglyphic inscriptions on inner face of enclosure wall, Temple of Horus, Edfu.

102. *Granite Horus falcon, Temple of Horus, Edfu.*

Sources and Further Reading

General

Baines, J., and Málek, J. *Atlas of Ancient Egypt*
    (New York, 1980).

Bowman, Alan K. *Egypt After the Pharaohs* (London, 1986).

Cerny, J. *Ancient Egyptian Religion* (London, 1952).

D'Auria, S., Lacovara, P., and Roehrig, Catherine H.
    Mummies and Magic: The Funerary Arts of Ancient Egypt
    (Museum of Fine Arts: Boston, 1988).

Edwards, I. E. S., et al., eds. *Cambridge Ancient History*, I–III,
    rev. ed. (Cambridge, 1970–82).

Fagan, B. *The Rape of the Nile* (New York, 1975).

Kitchen, K. A. *The Pharaoh Triumphant: The Life and
    Times of Ramesses II* (Mississauga, Canada, and

Porter, B. and Moss, R. L. B. *Topographical Bibliography of
    Ancient Egyptian Hieroglyphic Texts, Reliefs, and Paintings*,
    7 vols. (Oxford 1927–51); 2nd ed. (Oxford,
    1960–72).

Redford, D. *Pharaonic King-Lists, Annals and Day Books:
    A Contribution to the Egyptian Sense of History*
    (Mississauga, Canada, 1986).

Romer, J. *Valley of the Kings* (New York, 1981).

Vandier, J. *Manuel d'archéologie égyptienne*, 4 vols.
    (Paris, 1952–64).

GUIDEBOOKS

Baedeker's "Egypt," rev. ed. (Prentice Hall Press:
    New York, n.d.).

Murnane, W. *The Guide to Ancient Egypt* (New York, 1983).

Seton-Williams, V., and Stocks, P. *Blue Guide, Egypt*
    (New York, 1988).

WRITING AND LITERATURE

Davies, W. V. *Egyptian Hieroglyphs*
    (Berkeley and Los Angeles, 1987).

Gardner, Alan H. *Egyptian Grammer*, 3rd ed.
    (Oxford, 1957).

Lichtheim, M. *Ancient Egyptian Literature:
    A Book of Readings*, Vol. I–III (Berkeley, 1973–80).

Simpson, W. K., ed. *The Literature of Ancient Egypt*
    (New Haven and London, 1972).

Art and Architecture

Aldred, C. *Egyptian Art* (New York and Toronto, 1980).

Davies, Nina M., and Gardiner, Alan H.
    Ancient Egyptian Paintings, 3 vols. (Chicago, 1936).

Edwards, I. E. S. *The Pyramids of Egypt*, rev. ed.
    (London, 1985).

Lange, K., and Hirmer, M. *Egypt* (New York, 1968).

Mekhitarian, A. *Egyptian Painting* (Geneva, 1978).

Smith, W. S. *The Art and Architecture of Ancient Egypt*, rev. ed.
    by W. K. Simpson (New York, 1981).

DAILY LIFE

Bierbrier, M. *The Tomb Builders of the Pharaohs*
    (London, 1982).

Cerny, J. *A Community of Workmen at Thebes in the
    Ramesside Period* (Cairo, 1973).

James, T. G. H. *Pharaoh's People: Scenes from Life in
    Imperial Egypt* (London, 1984).

Montet, P. *Everyday Life in Egypt in the Days of
    Ramesses the Great* (Philadelphia, 1981).

Romer, J. *Ancient Lives: Daily Life in Egypt of the Pharaohs*
    (New York, 1984).

———. *Ancient Lives: The Story of the Pharaoh's Tombmakers*
    (London, 1984).